ECONOMIC ANALYSIS OF PROPE

POLITICAL ECONOMY OF INSTITUTIONS AND DECISIONS

Editors
Professor James Alt, Washington University in St. Louis
Professor Douglass North, Washington University in St. Louis

Other books in the series
Gary W. Cox, *The Efficient Secret*
Mathew D. McCubbins and Terry Sullivan (eds.), *Congress: Structure and Policy*

ECONOMIC ANALYSIS OF PROPERTY RIGHTS

YORAM BARZEL

CAMBRIDGE
UNIVERSITY PRESS

Published by the Press Syndicate of the University of Cambridge
The Pitt Building, Trumpington Street, Cambridge CB2 1RP
40 West 20th Street, New York, NY 10011-4211, USA
10 Stamford Road, Oakleigh, Victoria 3166, Australia

First published 1989
Reprinted 1991, 1993

Printed in the United States of America

Library of Congress Cataloging-in-Publication Data
Barzel, Yoram.
Economic analysis of property rights / Yoram Barzel.
p.   cm. – (Political economy of institutions and decisions)
Bibliography: p.
Includes index.
ISBN 0-521-36409-4. – ISBN 0-521-36704-2 (pbk.)
1. Property. 2. Right of property. I. Title. II. Series.
HB701.B37   1989
333.3–dc19   88–27026
                                                          CIP

British Library Cataloguing in Publication Data
Barzel, Yoram
Economic analysis of property rights
1. Property rights. Philosophical
perspectives
I. Title
323.4'6'01

ISBN 0-521-36409-4 hardback
ISBN 0-521-36704-2 paperback

To my parents

Contents

Series editors' preface

The Cambridge series on the Political Economy of Institutions and Decisions is built around attempts to answer two central questions: How do institutions evolve in response to individual incentives, strategies, and choices; and how do institutions affect the performance of political and economic systems? The scope of the series is comparative and historical rather than international or specifically American, and the focus is positive rather than normative.

In this book Yoram Barzel brings to fruition an original theory of property rights. In the tradition of Ronald Coase, he provides a unified structure to analyze exchange, the formation of rights, and organization. The approach, emphasizing non-market constraints, is applicable to non-market as well as market economies, to the allocation of resources within organizations as well as by voting.

Because of the costliness of measuring accurately all of an asset's attributes, rights are never fully delineated and property is consequently in danger of appropriation by others – not just by theft but also by excessive choosing, adverse selection, free riding, and shirking. Individuals incur transaction costs when they allocate resources and organize activities in order to enhance rights over their own assets and when they exchange in order to enhance their wealth. But they also spend and dissipate resources in order to capture a larger share of the gains. Barzel's analysis of these processes generates predictions of the contract forms that will be adopted under differing circumstances. A major implication is that in the face of imperfectly delineated rights, transactors willingly subject themselves to constraints.

The study argues that transactors adopt non-market constraints in order to lower the costs of exchange and that implementing and policing of restraints require organization. The firm, which reassigns rights among resource owners, is characterized by wage contracts and is the primary form of organization within a market economy. Resource owners choose to operate within the firm when it is difficult to delineate rights over output. When ouput is costly to measure, the wage contract with associated incentives and disincentives can yield, net of cost, a more valuable product than self-employment would have produced. The equity capital of the firm takes on ownership functions by guaranteeing the output and constraining the actions of its employed resources.

The discussion in this book is largely in the context of a market economy, but the approach has broad implications for any type of economy. It provides not only new insights into understanding of economic activity but also new building blocks for overhauling and restructuring microeconomic theory.

Preface

The intellectual content of "property rights," a term that has enchanted and occasionally mesmerized economists, seems to lie within the jurisdiction of the legal profession. Consistent with their imperialist tendencies, however, economists have also attempted to appropriate it. Both disciplines can justify their claims, since the term is given different meanings on different occasions. Perhaps economists should initially have coined a term distinct from the one used for legal purposes, but by now the cost of doing so is too high. I attempt, however, to make clear the meaning I give to "property rights" and to demonstrate why property rights so defined are an appropriate subject for economic analysis.

The material of the book is at the heart of a course I have taught in recent years. Undergraduate students take my approach in stride. Graduate students often vigorously resist my dissatisfaction with the zero transaction costs model; converting them is, however, rewarding. This book is influenced by the diverse classroom reactions. It is an attempt to appeal both to those with little training in economics and to specialists.

I am grateful to my former students Douglas Allen and Dean Lueck and to my colleague Paul Heyne, who read early drafts of the book and forced me to reformulate many of my ideas and to clarify their presentation. Douglass North, who supported the project from its infancy, also read the entire manuscript and made numerous valuable suggestions. Victor Goldberg and Levis Kochin provided useful comments as well. I also thank Elizabeth Case and my daughter Tamar for excellent editing; they demonstrated that clear writing enhances clear thinking. Finally, I wish to thank the Earhart Foundation for financial support.

I

Introduction: The property rights model

In the slave societies of the American South and of the West Indies, slaves persistently – albeit rarely – bought their contracts from their owners in order to redeem themselves from slavery. In these societies, as in others, the law afforded owners nearly absolute rights over their slaves and granted the slaves themselves no legal rights; consequently slaves were not legally entitled to own the property necessary for self-purchase. There was no legal barrier or authority to stand in the way of owners' owning both slave *and* freedom money. Nevertheless, self-purchase whereby slaves acquired property rights to their own labor did occur.

Because transacting is costly, as an economic matter property rights are never fully delineated. In the case of slaves, even though they were legally their owners' property, owners had to spend resources to induce their slaves to produce, and even then slaves seldom produced to their ultimate capacity. Thus slave ownership itself was never absolute, despite the slaves' lack of legal protection. Owners were able to enhance the value of their property through *granting* slaves some ownership rights in exchange for services the owners valued even more. Hence slaves were owners too, and could on occasion buy their freedom. As elaborated upon in Chapter 6, the study of property rights and of the costs of transacting can yield an explanation of why slaves were able to buy their freedom; such explanations may be tested against the facts. The property rights model I develop in this book can provide explanations of an array of such arrangements, which standard economic theory cannot successfully address, from identifying the reasons behind the choice between wage and piece-rate contracts to pinpointing the conditions under which charity is more efficient than profit-seeking behavior.

In the remainder of this chapter I shall define "property rights" and sketch the framework to be used in this book. In Chapter 2 the examination of the gasoline shortage in the 1970s illustrates the usefulness and importance of the property rights framework and familiarizes the reader with its mechanics. Chapters 3 and 4 present the property rights model and its main organizational implications. Chapters 5 through 9 expand the model and apply it to various problems including rights formation, slavery, and resource allocation in non-market settings, and Chapter 10 recapitulates.

THE INHERENT DIFFICULTY OF
DELINEATING RIGHTS FULLY

Property rights of individuals over assets consist of the rights, or the powers, to consume, obtain income from, and alienate these assets. Obtaining income from and alienating assets require exchange; exchange is the mutual ceding of rights. Legal rights, as a rule, enhance economic rights, but the former are neither necessary nor sufficient for the existence of the latter. The rights people have over assets (including themselves and other people) are not constant; they are a function of their own direct efforts at protection, of other people's capture attempts, and of government protection. The last condition is effected primarily through the police and the courts.[1] Squatters' rights to the land they occupy are less secure than those of legal owners not because they lack deeds but because less police protection is expected for such holdings. As defined here, property rights are not absolute and can be changed by individuals' actions; such a definition, then, is useful in the analysis of resource allocation. Economists' past failure to exploit the property rights notion in the analysis of behavior probably stems from their tendency to consider rights as absolute.

The concept of property rights is closely related to that of transaction costs. I define transaction costs as the costs associated with the transfer, capture, and protection of rights. If it is assumed that for any asset each of these costs is rising and that both the full protection and the full transfer of rights are prohibitively costly, then it follows that rights are never complete, because people will never find it worthwhile to gain the entire potential of "their" assets. In order that the rights to an asset be complete, or be perfectly delineated, both its owner and other individuals potentially interested in the asset must possess full knowledge of all its valued properties. With full knowledge, the transfer of rights to an asset can be readily effected. Conversely, when rights are perfectly delineated, product information must be costless to obtain, and the (relevant) costs of transacting must then be zero.

---

[1] The distinction sometimes made between property rights and human rights is spurious. Human rights are simply part of people's property rights. Human rights may be difficult to protect or to exchange, but so are rights to many other assets. See Alchian and Allen (1977, p. 114).

The property rights model

When transaction costs are positive, rights to assets cannot be perfectly delineated. The attributes of such assets are not fully known to prospective owners and are often not known to the current owner either. The transfer of assets entails costs resulting from both parties' attempts to determine what the valued attributes of these assets are and from the attempt by each to capture those attributes that, because of the prohibitive costs, remain poorly delineated.[2] Exchanges that otherwise would be attractive may be forsaken because of such exchange costs.

An illustration of the costliness of exchanging rights and their effect on resource allocation stems from the draft of college football players by the National Football League (NFL). Drafting is the acquisition by one team of the exclusive negotiation rights for the services of a player, inclusive of the right to transfer to any NFL team. Every year, the twenty-eight NFL teams select eligible college players in a predetermined sequence. It would seem that the team with the right to, say, the twentieth selection would select the player among those not yet drafted who is most valuable to any of the teams. Given the diversity of both players and teams, the probability that the team with the right to the twentieth selection will also be the one placing its highest value on any of the remaining players is the same as any other team's, that is, one in twenty-eight. Were the costs of exchange among teams low, the probability of that player's being traded would then be twenty-seven in twenty-eight. The observed trading frequency of newly drafted players, however, is much lower than a low transaction cost model predicts. This cost of transacting, at least, does seem to be considerable.

What underlies this costliness of transacting? What are the factors that prevent people from realizing the full value of their assets? Commodities have many attributes whose levels vary from one specimen of a commodity to another. The measurement of these levels is too costly to be comprehensive or entirely accurate. How difficult it is to obtain full information in the face of variability fundamentally determines how difficult it is to delineate rights. Because it is costly to measure commodities fully, the potential of wealth capture is present in every exchange. The opportunity for wealth capture is equivalent to finding property in the public domain; in every exchange, then, some wealth spills over into the public domain, and individuals spend resources to capture it. Whereas people always expect to gain from exchange, they also always spend resources on capture. Individuals maximize their (expected) net gains, the gains from exchange as conventionally perceived net of the cost of effecting exchange.

The sale of cherries illustrates the phenomenon of wealth capture. Obvious problems of information present themselves when cherries are

[2]Similar considerations, not elaborated on here, apply to the protection of assets.

3

exchanged. Customers must spend resources in order to determine whether a store's cherries are worth buying and in order to determine which particular cherries to buy. Store owners who allow customers to pick and choose cannot easily prevent them from eating cherries after they have already decided whether or not to buy them, nor can they prevent customers' careless handling of cherries. Indeed, the process of picking and choosing itself allows wealth capture in the form of excess choosing.[3] Some of the cherries' attributes, then, are placed in the public domain. The high cost of information results in transaction costs: costs that would not arise were the owner and the consumer of cherries the same person. If information about the cherries were costless, their initial owner would not have to relinquish any rights; and pilfering, damage, and excess choosing would be avoided. In reality, such public domain problems are unavoidable; people can take steps, however, to reduce the associated losses.

DIVIDED OWNERSHIP OF COMMODITIES

Net gains from exchange can often be increased if the original owners of commodities transfer only subsets of the commodities' attributes and retain the rest. Exchange that takes this form results in divided property rights for single commodities: Two or more individuals may own distinct attributes of the same commodity. As elaborated in Chapters 4 and 7, restrictions on the owners' behavior may be imposed in order to enhance the separation of their individual rights. Incomplete separation makes attributes common property, relinquishing them to the public domain; if they are in the public domain, resources are spent on their capture.

Not only is ownership of commodities often divided; ownership of organizations may be divided as well.[4] Physical operations within, and on the fringe of, an organization such as a firm usually involve many commodities and correspondingly many attributes. Several individuals share in ownership of the attributes, each owning alone, or with others, some subset of these. Stockholders own some of these attributes, but definitely not all of them. For instance, a firm (or, more accurately, its stockholders) that has a service contract for a copier to which it has the title does not fully own the copier. The firm is not the only party that gains when the copier performs well and loses when it does not. The service supplier is the residual claimant from the servicing operation, gaining if it provides good service and losing if the service is poor, and is thus part owner of the

[3]Barzel (1982).

[4]Alchian (1965) recognizes that ownership of commodities and of organizations may be divided. Posner (1986) discusses property rights and notes that ownership can be divided.

copier. In addition, the copier manufacturer is liable for certain damages caused by the copier, and employees who are able to use the copier privately without charge are also part owners, since, in practice, they have a claim on some of the copier's output. Here, too, restrictions may serve to separate rights and prevent free rides. In Chapter 7 it is shown that such restrictions do not necessarily attenuate rights; instead, they may enhance them.

FACTORS THAT AFFECT
THE ALLOCATION OF OWNERSHIP

The rights to receive the income flow generated by an asset are a part of the property rights over that asset. The greater is others' inclination to affect the income flow from someone's asset without bearing the full costs of their actions, the lower is the value of the asset. The maximization of the net value of an asset, then, involves that ownership or ownership pattern that can most effectively constrain uncompensated exploitation. The kind of ownership pattern to emerge depends on the variability of such assets.

The rights to an asset generating a flow of service are relatively easy to ensure when the flow can be readily ascertained, because it is easy to impose a charge commensurate with the level of service exchanged. Therefore, when the flow is *known* and *constant,* it is easiest to ensure that rights are also certain. If the flow is *variable* but is fully *predictable*, rights are still easy to ensure, as they are if the flow is not certain but is *unalterable*. It is evident, then, that, given the mean outcome, variability and uncertainty may reduce the value of the asset but need not affect the certainty of ownership.

When the flow of income from an asset may be affected by the exchange parties, ensuring ownership over it is problematic. When the income stream is variable and not fully predictable, it is costly to determine whether the flow is what it should have been in any particular case. Consequently it is also costly to determine whether part of the income stream has been captured by the exchange parties. The exchange parties will engage in wealth-consuming capture activities because they expect to gain from them. The delineation of ownership is problematic, then, when the income stream from the exchanged property is subject to random fluctuations and when both parties can gain by affecting that income stream.

A special case of great importance to understanding the circumstances under which ownership can be ensured arises when only one of two exchange parties can affect the income flow. Making the person who can affect the flow bear full responsibility for her or his actions ensures that

5

ownership becomes secure. Such a person, being the "residual claimant" to an outcome that only she or he can influence, is the full-fledged owner of the asset.

As a rule, both exchange parties can affect the service flow generated by exchanged assets, a fact that prevents ownership from being fully secure. For instance, the income stream generated by a rented car depends, in part, on how smoothly the car operates. Since used and even new cars are not identical to one another, they are not expected to run equally smoothly. A smooth ride is an attribute that both the owner and the renter can affect. A renter will find it expensive to determine to what extent the smooth ride of the rental car results from its character and to what extent it results from the care given to servicing it; similarly, the owner cannot tell how much the smoothness of the renter car's ride has deteriorated because of the way it has been driven and how much it has deteriorated because of its character. As a result, the owner may get away from skimping on servicing rental cars – doing less of it than owner-drivers would – and renters may be less careful with rented cars than they would be with their own. Each party expects such behavior of the other. Therefore, the demand function for rented cars adjusts for the effects of inadequate servicing, and the supply function adjusts for the effects of careless driving. The net gain in using the rental market, then, is less than it would be were the two parties to exercise greater care. If the smoothness of operations were costlessly measurable, the effect of each transactor on that attribute could be easily determined and accurately charged for. In reality, assessing such marginal charges accurately is prohibitively expensive, and (maximizing) owners will not choose to exercise their rights fully. Some of the income stream, then, is left in the public domain and is partly recaptured by the exchanging parties, who act differently than owner-users would. Whereas rights cannot economically be fully defined when both exchange parties are able to affect the outcome, only one pattern of ownership does maximize the net income from the asset (and thus its value to its original owner). The general principle determining the maximizing allocation of ownership is that the greater a party's inclination to affect the mean income an asset can generate, the greater is the share of the residual that party assumes.

The nominal owner of an asset may seem to have the right to the income the asset can generate. When the highest income the asset can generate requires exchange, some of the income potential will be used up in the process of effecting the exchange. The net income an asset will generate, then, *depends* on the delineation of rights, that is, on how secure rights are over it. In the case described earlier where only one person can affect the income from an asset, it is only when that person becomes owner of the asset that rights are perfectly well defined, and it is only then that the income is maximized. To say that when rights are well defined income is maximized regardless of who has these rights is meaningless, because, as discussed in Chapter 4, only that assignment of rights that is consistent with maximum income delineates rights perfectly clearly.

THE RELATIONSHIP BETWEEN INDIVIDUALS' RIGHTS AND ECONOMIC ORGANIZATIONS

Contracts govern the exchange of property rights and are central to the study of such rights. Some contracting parties consist of individuals acting on their own behalf. Others consist of pairs of organizations such as firms, governments, clubs, and families. In addition, there are contracts between individuals and such organizations. Because individuals' objectives are relatively clear, it is useful to define *all* property rights as rights possessed by individuals. Ultimately, individuals always interact with other individuals, regardless of whether one or both interacting parties represent organizations in some capacity. The payments supermarket shoppers make for merchandise can be viewed as exchanges between individuals and an organization – between customers and the store. Such relationships, however, can always be reduced to the individual level. Here, we consider the relationship between the cashier and the customers, on the one hand, and between the cashier and the store manager, on the other. A cashier in a store has the right to collect money from customers who buy in the store. The cashier, of course, does not usually retain customers' payments; rather, in exchange for an hourly wage, the cashier cedes to the store manager rights over her or his time as well as rights over the cash received from customers. The manager's relationships with other individuals such as the store owners involve, in turn, other sets of exchanged rights. The functioning of any organization can be similarly reduced to the ceding of various rights from one individual associated with it to another.

The assumption of individual maximization, and in particular the assumption that individuals maximize the value of their rights, is useful not only directly in the analysis of individuals' behavior but also indirectly as the assumption underlying the functioning of organizations. The study of private property rights, then, can be applied to all organizations – indeed, to all societies. Individual maximization implies that whenever individuals perceive that certain actions will enhance the value of their rights, they undertake such actions. This always applies, whether the individuals operate in markets, in firms, in families, in tribes, in government, or in any other organization.

OPERATIONAL FEATURES OF
THE PROPERTY RIGHTS MODEL

The exchange value of an asset is a function of the gross income it can generate and of the costs of measuring and policing its exchange. These costs also determine the pattern and the degree of ownership. The ownership of assets' attributes is expected to gravitate into the hands of those people who are most inclined to affect the income flows the attributes can generate. The gross income stream (the market value of the flow of services) an asset can generate, the value of the contributions of different individuals, and the costs of policing and measuring the attributes of the asset determine both how strictly rights to it will be delineated and what its ownership pattern will be. Since these and similar magnitudes are measurable, the ingredients necessary for an operational theory of property rights are available. These operational features also apply to the analysis of constraints.

Because of the costliness of delineating and policing rights, opportunities arise for some people to capture others' wealth. As demonstrated in Chapter 3, these opportunities arise from people's ability to overuse and to underprovide unpriced attributes when exchanging with each other. Exchange partners may impose restrictions on each other in order to reduce the level of undesired behavior. Consequently, property rights, particularly the right to consume (what appears to be) one's property, are often subjected to constraint. The character and incidence of the constraints are predictable. Analysis of the constraints on property rights, therefore, can help make the study of these rights operational.

THE PROPERTY RIGHTS APPROACH VERSUS
THE WALRASIAN MODEL

The significance of the study of property rights results from the fact of positive transaction costs. On the other hand, in the Walrasian, perfectly competitive, model, rights are perfectly delineated and transaction costs are zero. It is useful, then, briefly to contrast the models of the positive costs of transaction with the Walrasian model. A fundamental difference between the two concerns the role of prices. In the Walrasian model, costlessly determined prices suffice for all allocation problems; but costly transacting requires non-price allocation methods and corresponding organizations.

When equilibrium is disturbed in the Walrasian model, a new equilibrium is instantaneously attained because, given zero transaction costs, the cost of adjustment is zero. In that model, a commodity is made up of strictly identical specimens, people are fully informed regarding the exchanged commodities, the terms of trade are always perfectly clear, and trade is instantaneous. As a result, no effort is required to effect exchange other than that to dispense the appropriate amount of cash. Prices alone always *suffice* to allocate resources to their highest-value uses.

In the Walrasian model, where prices are sufficient for efficient allocation, institutions are superfluous; firms, clubs, tribes, or families cannot enhance efficiency. Yet for a long time economists attempted to address questions of organization by what amounted to ad hoc tinkering with the Walrasian model. Only recently have people begun to take notice of the inevitable inconsistencies in such an approach. The transaction cost model used here explicitly explores the effects of positive information cost on behavior and on organization.

When equilibrium is disturbed in a positive transaction cost world, price adjustment is not expected to be instantaneous. As long as prices are not fully adjusted to new conditions, the quantities demanded are not, in general, equal to those supplied. Nevertheless, it is possible to determine how equilibrium will be attained. Where transaction costs are positive, a whole array of activities is required to effect exchange; cash with which to pay the pecuniary price is helpful but definitely not sufficient. Because of the complexity of exchange, the parties have many opportunities to alter their behavior from one transaction to another. To illustrate, consider first some of the activities required to effect purchases in stores. Buyers must decide, among other things, whether to shop during the busiest hours or at off-peak times; they must identify the location of the desired merchandise; see, by themselves or with the help of the sellers, if the items they seek are available; and determine if they are of the appropriate quality. They must select the specimens they think are best; ascertain the price, sometimes after haggling; and pay (not necessarily in cash). In addition, they may have to take care of warranties and, on occasion, exchange the merchandise. Effecting purchases, then, involves an elaborate set of operations. More important, the costs and valuations of most of these operations can be altered. For instance, at any particular time a seller may be out of an item that is usually in plentiful supply, or the seller may unexpectedly help carry the merchandise to customers' cars. When the market-clearing price changes but the nominal price does not, buyers and sellers have many margins with regard to which they may still adjust. They can gain from such adjustments, and wealth maximization implies that adjustments will be forthcoming.

Sellers can adjust to a price that is lower than the market-clearing level along various margins. A seller who is in control of the quality of the merchandise or of the number of cashiers per customer will adjust along such margins. Thus supermarkets tend to reduce the speed of service at rush hours. In general, sellers who choose not to adjust prices or who are prevented from adjusting them may still adjust along other margins. Given wealth maximization, the margins along which they will adjust and the corresponding effects on resource allocation are predictable.

The analysis of non-price adjustments or of property rights need not be restricted to the market sector in an economy or to market economies; on the contrary, the results of such analysis apply everywhere. They are as applicable to China during the Red Guard era as they are to Hong Kong or to tribes entirely without a market system. Application, of course, requires knowledge of the underlying constraints, and such knowledge may be harder to come by in some systems than in others. Property rights notions are usually applied to the capitalist market system only; actually, the property rights approach is at its most useful (and the Walrasian model is at its least useful) in systems in which market prices are least used and least allowed to adjust. In Chapter 8 I will discuss briefly the applicability of property rights tools to a non-price economy.

Virtually all governments play a major role with regard to property rights; they also own properties and participate directly in economic activities. In addition, governments are heavily involved with adjudicating and enforcing contracts. A comprehensive analysis of the roles of government is beyond the scope of the present project. These roles of government will be touched upon in Chapter 8, but largely in the process of analyzing the behavior of individuals and enterprises. Customs and mores seem to be additional non-price factors that affect the allocation of resources. However, the effects of these factors on behavior and on the enforcement of contracts will be ignored: Although the factors to be considered are allowed to change, customs and mores, like tastes, are assumed to be stable, and accordingly have no effect on the margin.

THE DISTINCTIVENESS OF
THE PROPERTY RIGHTS APPROACH

An enormous amount of literature written in the last quarter century departs from the Walrasian, costless transacting, model. This literature, in which the costs of information play a major role, is diverse, and thus far no single model has stood out as the most useful one. Different approaches with a bewildering array of names proliferate: "agency theory," or the "principal-agent model"; "market signaling"; "rent seeking"; "bounded rationality"; "asymmetric information"; and "contract theory." It is difficult to determine the precise differences between, and sometimes within, these approaches, because as a rule many assumptions are only implicit. Moreover, the empirical work in the area is too meager to help distinguish among them.

I shall make no attempt to sort out these models. I shall offer, however, a few highly stylized suggestions as to why I find models such as these that do not focus on property rights to be less appealing than the property rights model. It should be made clear, though, that the differences among the models often seem more a matter of emphasis than a reflection of different fundamental assumptions.

The "agency theory" starting point is that principals' maximizing attempts are frustrated by agents whose objectives do not coincide with their own.[5] The asserted asymmetry between the two parties is likely to divert attention from the reciprocity of, and perhaps even from the gains from, exchange. The "rent seeking" approach tends to ignore almost to a fault gains from exchange; it concentrates on people's efforts to capture wealth from each other and neglects opportunities to gain through avoiding waste.[6]

The problems inherent in the models based on asset specificity and on the opportunistic capture of quasi rent are very different.[7] Such models usually deal with variables that are exceedingly difficult to observe and to measure. The proxies required to make such models operational are even farther removed from the desired variables than is usually the case in economics. Thus it is particularly difficult to determine precisely what it is that empirical tests confirm or refute. "Market signaling," like rent seeking, emphasizes exploitation rather than maximization;[8] and as with the asset specificity model, it is difficult to formulate empirical counterparts to the variables the theory suggests.

In contrast, contracts that delineate and reassign ownership are central to the property rights approach. The study of contracts formed by maximizing individuals, and of the performance such contracts induce, tends to maintain a close correspondence between theoretical variables and their empirical counterparts. Knight (1924) was apparently the first to point out explicitly the economic role of property rights, and Gordon's (1954) thrust is similar. Coase (1960), Alchian (1965), and Cheung (1969) bring operational elements to the analysis. The relative ease of rendering the property rights model operational is made clear in the following chapters.

The property rights model developed in Chapters 3 and 4 is used in

[5]Ross (1973) and Jensen and Meckling (1976) are early proponents of agency theory.

[6]Tullock (1967) and Krueger (1974) started the rent-seeking literature.

[7]Williamson (1975) and Klein, Crawford, and Alchian (1978) initiated the notion of the capture of quasi rent.

[8]This approach had been initiated by Arrow (1973) and Spence (1973).

Chapter 5 to follow through on Demsetz's (1967) and Umbeck's (1977) embryonic contributions on rights formation. In Chapter 5 I attempt to show that the property rights model is useful in predicting when new rights will be created and when existing rights will be placed in the public domain. I also argue that such changes pervade economic activity.[9]

[9]Another distinction of my study, although this need not be unique to the property rights approach, is that I take no account of problems of risk aversion; all my attempts to explain behavior proceed under the assumption of risk neutrality. As is shown in Chapter 3, there is much to be gained and little to be lost by assuming people to be risk-neutral.

2

The public domain:
rationing by waiting and price controls

This chapter consists primarily of an elaborate example – the 1970s price controls on gasoline – that illustrates the usefulness and power of the property rights framework. Chapter 1 contains a property rights proposition central to this book: Unless property rights are perfectly delineated, which, given positive transaction costs, they never are, some valued properties will always be in the public domain. In this chapter the nature of maximization as affected by properties in the public domain is examined and the actual resolutions of several public domain issues are analyzed. Because an analysis of rationing by waiting offers a convenient introduction to the subject of property rights, I will initially concentrate, though briefly, on such an analysis; I will subsequently present the more detailed analysis of maximization under price controls, which brings out major features of the substance and the mechanics of property rights.

RATIONING BY WAITING

The rationing by waiting model used here, which is stripped of many real-world features, is most elementary. Using this model makes it easy to concentrate on the public domain issue and ignore peripheral problems. I will use the results of this basic analysis in the subsequent analysis of the 1973–75 price controls on gasoline.

When the government provides commodities at a zero pecuniary price and makes them available on a first-come first-served basis, commodities are allocated strictly by the order in which individuals join the queue, and ultimately by the amount of time individuals spend waiting in line. Even though orderly queues are often encountered, they should not be taken for granted, as the following example illustrates. Suppose it is publicly announced that a package containing $1 million is to be given to the first in line at a particular place. It might seem that the first person to hear the announcement would rush to the site and wait for the package to arrive.

13

If, however, no policing of the line is to be provided, the ultimate owner of the $1 million is likely to be someone with an armored truck and a machine gun. In the absence of policing, the first person to hear such an announcement will probably not bother to join the queue unless she or he is able to compete effectively with owners of machine guns.

The specific nature of restrictions (in the preceding example, first-come first-served and no policing) delineates the margins of competition – in this case firepower rather than time. The queue will be orderly only if the appropriate restrictions are placed upon it. Such restrictions seem to be applied often, and orderly rationing by waiting is a common occurrence. I will assume that the queue is policed enough to be orderly.

The mechanics developed in price theory texts can readily be used to determine the properties of the first-come first-served allocation. On the supply side, the government supplies a fixed quantity of a good. On the demand side, the only change from the textbook mechanics I make in my analysis is to exchange commodities for time rather than for money. Given the fixed supply, forces of demand determine the equilibrium price per unit of the good being distributed in terms of the amount of time spent by individuals in the queue. Almost anything that can be said about money in the standard case can be applied to time when allocation is by waiting.[1]

One evident and important difference between rationing by dollars and rationing by time, however, is that allotment of dollars across individuals differs from the corresponding allotment of time. If there is a good whose waiting time per unit is five minutes, if waiting is the only method of acquiring the good, and if the good cannot be traded, then a person will stand in line to obtain additional units of the good until the value of five minutes of his time reaches the value of one extra unit of the good. For example, when the value of the individual's time is $12 per hour (or $1 for five minutes), he will continue to rejoin the line to obtain another unit of the good as long as his marginal valuation of the good exceeds $1. If the price of the good becomes $1 instead of five minutes, the analysis proceeds along standard lines. Given that the good cannot be traded, the individuals who ultimately get the good in the original case, however, are those who value it most in time rather than in money.

Changes in the rules governing distribution of the good can be accommodated easily by this model of rationing by waiting. For instance, there is no reason to assume that the given commodity will be doled out in fixed batches. There are other possible rules governing its distribution: Individuals may be allowed as much of it as they desire; access to the line may be limited to once per period or allowed any number of times; and

[1] Barzel (1974, pp. 73–95).

once the commodity is obtained, trading it may be permitted. Each rule constitutes a distinct way of allocating rights to the good.

This basic analysis of rationing by waiting yields one key result: A commodity announced to be free is effectively placed in the public domain and is of no value until ownership is established. Establishing ownership requires that an individual fulfill certain criteria – in the example here, the criterion is to spend five minutes in a queue. Acquisition of the commodity consumes real resources over and above the resources used in production. In the example, ownership of one already produced unit is established by spending five minutes in a queue. Whatever the method by which rights are acquired – and such methods differ from case to case – it is generally true that resources must be spent to gain possession of commodities in the public domain, and that individual maximization applies here no less than to conventional exchange.

PRICE CONTROL ANALYSIS

How are property rights allocated to a commodity that is sold at prices below the market equilibrium level? In the model of rationing by waiting, queuing is the means by which ownership is established. Rationing by waiting can be viewed as a special case of price control.

Real-world price controls differ from rationing by waiting in two important ways. First, whereas in the price control analysis all that is required is that the controlled price be lower than the equilibrium price, in the rationing by waiting model I assume that the (money) price is zero.[2] Second, whereas in the rationing by waiting model I assume that competition can occur only through queuing, in the price control analysis that assumption is not always valid.

In the rationing by waiting model, individuals acquire rights to the rationed commodity by spending the appropriate amount of time in the queue. Under price controls, rights allocation is more complex, and the determination of how rights to an asset are actually allocated is essential in the analysis of the controls.[3] In the remainder of this chapter I analyze the early-1970s price controls on gasoline. Before beginning this analysis, however, it is worthwhile to look at a generic price control model.

In the generic model, it is assumed that competition initially emerges as queuing. Consider Figure 2.1, where D is the demand curve, S is the supply curve, the equilibrium price and quantity are represented by P^* and Q^*, and the control price is represented by P_C. Assuming that the control price is perfectly enforced, a discrepancy between quantity de-

---

[2] I focus on price ceilings – below equilibrium price controls – and ignore price floors – above equilibrium price controls.

[3] See Cheung (1974, pp. 53–71).

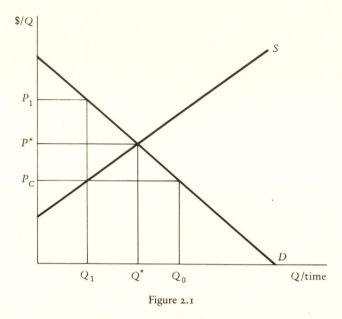

Figure 2.1

manded, Q_0, and quantity supplied, Q_1, known as "shortage," will arise. Sellers will only supply Q_1; Q_1, then, is the quantity available to consumers, a quantity for which they will be willing to pay P_1. Because consumers can pay P_C only in money, they will spend the difference $(P_1 - P_C)$ by waiting in line. For example, if $Q = 100$, $P_C = \$1$, $P_1 = \$2$, and the opportunity cost for consumers is $\$10$ per hour, then buyers in the aggregate will spend a total of $\$100$ in money and ten hours in time to purchase ten units.[4] Because queuing is the only margin of competition, this is the new equilibrium under the price control. As the discussion proceeds, various simplifying assumptions underlying the generic model will be dropped one at a time. It is essential, however, first to describe the control itself and its background.

The price controls

The Economic Stabilization Act of 1970 gave the president of the United States the authority to impose controls on prices. On August 15, 1971, President Richard Nixon imposed a ninety-day economywide freeze of prices at their May 1971 level. This freeze was known as Phase

[4] The area $(P_1 - P_C) \times Q_1$ in Figure 2.1 represents the dollar value of the time expenditure.

16

I of the price controls.[5] Phase II, which began on November 14, 1971, contained a less stringent set of price regulations, which did allow many firms to raise prices above Phase I levels when input costs increased. Gasoline prices, however, as well as the prices of heating oil, crude oil, and residual fuel, were effectively controlled at the Phase I level. Phase III, introduced on January 11, 1973, initially involved a voluntary form of the Phase II controls. On June 14, 1973, the Nixon administration imposed another economywide price freeze as part of Phase III. This freeze lasted until August 12, 1973, at which time Phase IV, the final phase, began. However, for the petroleum industry, including gasoline retailers, the Phase III freeze continued until September 6, 1973. Phase IV was essentially a period of gradual price deregulation, although petroleum products, including retail gasoline, were still subject to price controls.

For many commodities, the price controls caused such inconveniences as fewer sales made on credit, a smaller variety of goods available, and less frequent free delivery. As a rule, shortages did not arise. In the case of gasoline, the discrepancy between the controlled price and the market-clearing price that would have prevailed without the controls was not small enough to mask some of the effects of the price controls.[6] In the wake of the Arab–Israeli war that erupted on October 6, 1973, the Organization of Arab Petroleum Exporting Countries (OAPEC) restricted exports and raised the price of crude petroleum.[7] Prior to the war, the world price of crude oil had been around $3 a barrel. On October 16, OAPEC raised the price to nearly $5 per barrel, and on December 23 the price was raised to $11.561 per barrel.[8] This drastic price increase – more than threefold in nominal dollars – coupled with price controls led to shortages and queuing in the United States by December 1973. Some aspects of these shortages may conveniently be analyzed using the property rights model.

---

[5]Much of the information on the Nixon administration price controls comes from Kalt (1981) and Rockoff (1984). In the case of retail gasoline, prices were not explicitly controlled; instead, the margins, or markups, were controlled at various stages. Only the price of crude petroleum was controlled. (This information was provided by Bruce Peterson of the American Petroleum Institute and Del Fogelquist of the Western Oil and Gas Association.) The Cost of Living Council and the Internal Revenue Service were the primary agencies involved with policy and enforcement of the controls.

[6]The meaning of "small enough" is clarified in the last paragraph of this chapter.

[7]OAPEC is an influential subgroup within the Organization of Petroleum Exporting Countries (OPEC).

[8]The average per barrel regulated price of crude oil in the United States was $3.89 for 1973 and $6.87 for 1974. See *Statistical Abstract of the United States 1986*, p. 698.

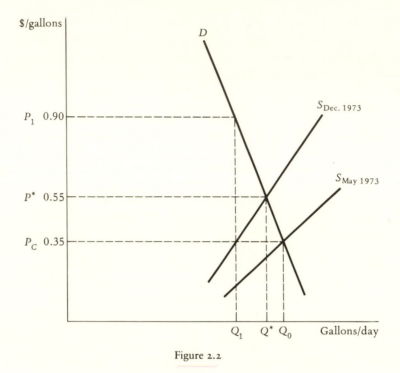

Figure 2.2

The gasoline transaction

Gasoline may appear to be a simple commodity. In the course of this chapter, however, it should become clear that gasoline transactions have numerous valued attributes. Because during the period of price controls market participants were able to alter the levels of attributes not controlled by the government, the actual allocation of property rights differed from that nominally specified by the controls. The examination of this price control episode brings out the strength of the property rights framework in suggesting areas for economic inquiry and in developing refutable implications.

Figure 2.2 depicts the change in circumstances in the gasoline market induced by the 1973 Arab–Israeli war. In May 1971 the price of regular gasoline was about 35 cents per gallon (P_C). The crude-oil price hike that resulted from the war caused a shift up and to the left in the supply of gasoline, from something like $S_{\text{May 1973}}$ to $S_{\text{Dec. 1973}}$, as depicted in Figure 2.2.[9]

[9]Control of the wholesale price of gasoline complicates, but does not change, the essence of the analysis.

In the absence of price controls, the market-clearing price would have been around 55 cents per gallon, P^*, after this decline in supply.[10] What effect did price controls have on the behavior of market participants? Prior to Cheung's work, the price control literature asserted that a shortage of $(Q_o - Q_1)$ would arise or that the typical consumer would acquire a fraction of the amount of gasoline desired.[11] However, the contention that the shortage would be borne proportionately, randomly, or arbitrarily ignores the postulate of wealth maximization; and in the process the concept of equilibrium was and is often ignored.

Wealth maximization implies that individuals will carry on an activity until, for the marginal unit, net gains are zero. The question that must be asked even when a price is controlled is: Can the buyer or the seller take additional steps to get or to provide another unit at a cost below the added gain? If the answer is yes, an equilibrium has not yet been reached. The notion of a "market-clearing" equilibrium requires that all individuals make whatever moves they wish to make given the existing property rights arrangement. Textbook analyses of a binding price ceiling that conclude that a shortage will exist ignore the possibility of adjustments and thus implicitly deny that individuals maximize if adjustments are available. The way in which margins of adjustment were exploited under gasoline price controls will be examined in the next few sections.

Preliminary considerations of property rights under controls

The Nixon administration could have exercised several options instead of, or in addition to, simply imposing price controls. As the shortage became severe, it could, for instance, have estimated Q_1 (Figure 2.1 or Figure 2.2) and issued coupons for that number of gallons. Had coupons been issued, rights to the purchase of gasoline would have been allocated; and because property rights would have been secure, people would not have needed to spend resources to acquire these rights. In fact, coupons were not issued, so the question at issue is: What property rights system prevailed under price controls?

Earlier, using Figure 2.1, I made the general statement that when the maximum price for a commodity is set at P_C, the quantity of it that will be available in the marketplace is Q_1. Underlying this statement are two important assumptions about property rights, one explicit and one implicit. The explicit assumption is that under price controls the sellers' right to set prices is restricted; here, sellers of gasoline were legally prohibited from selling it at any price above 35 cents per gallon. The implicit

[10]As controls were relinquished, the uncontrolled price of gasoline finally leveled off at around 55 cents per gallon in the summer of 1974.
[11]See Cheung (1974) for a review of this literature.

assumption is that sellers retain the right to provide whatever quantity they wish. Given the sellers' marginal cost curve and the control price of 35 cents per gallon, the maximizing quantity they would have offered was Q_1, as indicated in Figure 2.2. Consumers wished to purchase Q_0 at the control price, but this quantity had no operational relevance: No forces were present to yield this quantity. Q_1 was ultimately the quantity that was allocated among the consumers. P_1 is the maximum price that consumers would pay to purchase the (entire) quantity Q_1, which in Figure 2.2 is 90 cents per gallon of gasoline. Q_1, the quantity offered at P_C, was the quantity that consumers wanted to purchase at the higher price P_1. In reality, rationing by waiting turned out to be the equilibrating force, given that the maximum price sellers had the right to charge was lower than the one buyers were willing to pay.

Rationing of gasoline by waiting

Why did waiting lines for gasoline materialize in the fall of 1973? Shortages per se are not a cause for waiting, and the regulators had never formally adopted queuing as the method of allocating gasoline. It became clear, however, that queuing, although subject to various exceptions and added controls, was the only method of distribution that was going to be allowed.

Under controls, the actual pecuniary price per gallon of gasoline was positive – 35 cents. Although rationing by waiting was analyzed on the assumption that the pecuniary price is zero, as long as the controlled price of gasoline is held below the market-clearing price, the queuing analysis essentially applies. Gasoline, then, was placed in part in the public domain, and the queue served to establish rights over that unowned component. Gasoline sellers owned the property rights to 35 cents per gallon of gasoline, and buyers could acquire rights to the difference between P_1 and P_C (which in Figure 2.2 is 55 cents per gallon) by getting in the queue. If the wage rate of the marginal waiter had been $6 per hour (or 10 cents per minute), the market-clearing queue length would have been five and a half minutes per gallon.[12]

Given that buyers acquired gasoline by a combination of money and

---

[12] An important complication arises with regard to the mechanics of the queue. It makes a difference, for example, if gasoline is rationed by the gallon or by the tank. In most cases, gas was rationed by the (capacity of the) tank. A person who drove a car with a small tank could get less gasoline than someone whose car had a large tank. Since waiting time was independent of the size of the gas tank, savings associated with purchase size became more prominent, and consequently the expected frequency of people's running out of gas was higher. Independent of shortages, a person could save resources (time) by filling the tank less often, and people occasionally did run out of gas by postponing purchase too long. The expectation is that with price controls, people will run out of gas more often.

time, the conventional demand curve is somewhat misspecified. As usually formulated, it shows how much money people will pay for varying
amounts of gasoline when no waiting is required, but not how much they
will pay in terms of a combination of money and time. It is easy to
construct a modified demand curve in which the price is stated in minutes
per gallon, given that 35 cents per gallon must also be paid. Such a
demand curve displays marginal valuation in terms of time per unit over
and above 35 cents per unit. Compared with the conventional formulation, this type of demand curve varies across individuals, depending on
the opportunity cost of their time. Of two individuals who have identical
demand for gasoline but who differ in their opportunity cost of time, the
one with the low opportunity cost of time will always be able to outbid
the other once queuing becomes part of the price of gasoline. In what
follows, demand is assumed to account for the two components of price. I
will now return to the main problem.

The preceding discussion of the rights of sellers and of buyers brings
out the fact that the rights to the value of the gasoline were divided by
price controls. The sellers had the right to the value of the gasoline up to
the control price, and the buyers could acquire the right to the difference
between the control price and their marginal valuation by joining a
queue. By paying the control price plus the time price, the buyers could
obtain the property rights to a gallon of gasoline. Except for the fact that
buyers had to pay a pair of prices, the market for gasoline may be viewed
as having functioned normally. Indeed, there are many markets in which
both money and time prices are paid by the buyer. A person who insists
on eating lunch at noon in the cafeteria is charged a money price by the
cashier and faces a time price as well: waiting time. In this case, pecuniary
prices for commodities are fixed by the market. In the case of gasoline,
the money price was fixed by government.

What are the regulators regulating?

The preceding analysis contains many implicit assumptions that tag the
waiting price onto the control price. In the next few sections some of
these assumptions are altered in order to increase the correspondence
between the waiting model and the actual situation.

The approximate average price of gasoline in the United States in May
1971 was 35 cents per gallon, and in the analysis a single control price of
35 cents per gallon was used. Yet the gasoline price controls were based
on actual gasoline prices, which were subject to considerable variation.
Prices were lower at gas stations nearer to production centers, reflecting
lower transportation costs. Prices were higher for premium than for regular gasoline. Prices were lower at gas stations that used low prices as

promotional devices than at gas stations that used other means of promotion. Prices were lower at self-service stations. A self-service station selling regular gasoline at 34 cents per gallon in the summer of 1973 would have had to sell regular at a maximum price of 34 cents during price controls, and a full-service station selling regular at 38 cents during this period would have had its maximum price fixed at 38 cents.[13] A price control constitutes the assignment of property rights; assuming that the regulators could easily ascertain the actual base price and could easily enforce it, delineation was clear in one important respect: Each seller clearly knew what price he could legally charge. In other essential respects, however, delineation was less clear.

What exactly is it that one purchases in a gas station? "Gasoline" is not a sufficient answer. Like all transacted commodities, gasoline has a large number of valuable attributes. For example, when is it available? Is the gas station open nine hours per day or twenty-four hours per day? Is the octane rating 88 or 98? Is the gas station self-service or full-service? It is essential to have specific information about regulation of the attributes of gasoline before its effects can be adequately examined. Ambiguity surrounded the control of such attributes under price controls.

Much of the ambiguity in the scope of controls results directly from the great number and variability of attributes of gasoline. The attributes of gasoline transactions can be classified into those of the gasoline itself and those of the services provided with the gasoline. Gasoline is commonly graded as regular or as premium, depending on the octane rating; here I assume that under the controls premium gasoline had to have a minimum octane rating of 90.[14] Thus "premium gasoline" describes a range of products 90 octane and above, not a strictly defined single product. There are other variations among premium gasolines. For example, Exxon's premium gasoline had performance additives different from Shell's, and the premium gasoline sold in the Rocky Mountains was probably refined differently from that sold at sea-level locations. Price controls essentially ignored most of the variations in gasoline quality. Because it is prohibitively costly to define rights to all the valuable attributes of a commodity, it is not surprising that the control specifications were not fully detailed. Correspondingly, it is expected that regulations also consistently fail to address certain attributes specifically. Indeed, the real-world price con-

---

[13]Actually, it is difficult to figure out the precise price used by the regulators.

[14]Premium and regular grades are generally determined by industry standards through the American Petroleum Institute (API) and the American Society for Testing and Methods (ASTM). Bruce Peterson of the API reports that the standards are voluntary, although there are some state regulations, with varying degrees of enforcement. No single octane rating is specified to distinguish regular from premium; for purposes of the analysis I assume that premium gasoline must be at least 90 octane and regular can be any octane lower than that.

trols specified just the grade of gasoline and largely ignored other attributes, including attributes of the second type (kind of service provided).

When attributes subject to variability are incompletely specified, the affected parties, correspondingly, are allowed different amounts of leeway, each according to her or his particular circumstances. Consider the following illustration. Two stations, A and B, were selling premium gasoline in the summer of 1973. Station A sold 90-octane premium for 39 cents per gallon, and station B sold 92-octane premium for 43 cents. The lowest octane level at which a gasoline was still considered premium was 90; B could lower its octane from 92 to 90 while staying within the controller's definition of premium.[15] When price controls were imposed, A was allowed to sell premium for no more than 39 cents and B could sell premium for no more than 43 cents. As a result of the price controls, part of the rights to the value of the gasoline was placed in the public domain. In my initial analysis, in which gasoline was implicitly considered as a homogeneous commodity, it was seen that price controls effectively allowed the seller to retain the right to 35 cents per gallon and allowed buyers to capture the remaining value (which had been put in the public domain) by joining a queue. This conclusion must be reexamined in light of the opportunity to adjust the quality of the gasoline.

The regulation did not restrict sellers to the precise quality of gasoline they were selling during the spring of 1973. With product quality as a variable and with a regulation that did not specify all of the relevant quality attributes, property rights had become extremely murky by late 1973. Both station A and station B were required to maintain the octane level of their premium gasolines at no less than 90. Station A was restricted to a maximum price of 39 cents a gallon and to a minimum octaine level of 90; station B was restricted to the set minimum octane level but to a maximum price of 43 cents a gallon. Station B, then, could lower its octane to below pre-control levels and still sell the gasoline as premium for 43 cents. If gas stations had to pay refiners 2 cents per gallon for each unit increase in octane level, station B was able to save 4 cents per gallon of premium gasoline. As long as consumers were willing to pay more than 43 cents per gallon for premium gasoline (i.e., $P_1 > 0.43$), they were willing to pay the higher money price for B's gasoline, provided that the time price they had to pay was correspondingly less than for A's gasoline. Since the time price reflected acquiring rights from the public domain and was not transferred to anybody, there was no countervailing loss from the reduction in waiting time when buying B's gasoline. Station B, by being able to adjust gasoline quality without violating the regulation, could capture some of the value of the gasoline that seemed to end

[15] I am assuming that the retailer was in charge of gasoline quality, which because of price controls at the wholesale level, may not have been so.

up in the public domain as a result of price controls. The government's specification of rights played into the hands of station B.

Two tests of the preceding analysis follow. First, gasoline quality, in terms of octane levels, should have declined as sellers attempted to capture the value that was placed in the public domain. Second, the quantity of antiknock additives (substitutes for octane sold separately from gasoline) should have increased subsequent to the imposition of price controls.

I will now turn to an analysis of gas station services and the attendant impact of price controls. The type and level of services attached to the purchase of gasoline vary considerably from station to station. Full-service stations pump the gas, wash windshields, and provide clean restrooms; self-service stations provide little besides the gasoline itself. As it applied to gasoline, the price control regulation specified nothing about the level of services to be provided along with the gasoline. A simple illustration using two stations, which differ only in the level of services they provide, will serve to isolate the effects of this lack of specification. Station 1 sells regular gasoline for 33 cents per gallon and provides few extra services.[16] Station 2 sells the same regular gasoline for 36 cents, but provides 3 cents' worth of services per gallon in the form of pumping the gas, cleaning the windshield, and checking under thte hood. Once price controls are imposed, Station 1 can charge no more than 33 cents per gallon; Station 2 can charge no more than 36 cents. Station 2, like station B in the previous example, has an additional margin of adjustment not available to station 1. Station 2 can reduce its service level to zero, saving 3 cents per gallon in costs, and still sell gasoline for 36 cents, enabling it to avoid losing some of its wealth to the public domain. Consumers will buy all that station 2 can sell at 36 cents a gallon without service so long as the cost of waiting at station 1 exceeds 3 cents per gallon.

The available supply of gasoline declined during the era of price controls, and the number of stations selling it also got smaller. Those stations that had the greatest number of margins at which to adjust were able to tolerate the price control situation longer than those with fewer margins of adjustment. Because consumers would pay the same full price for the same product no matter where they made the purchase, they were indifferent between paying a higher money price and waiting less at the first kind of station and doing the reverse at the second kind. Thus, self-service or no-service stations, the ones having fewer margins at which to adjust to price controls, were expected to be among the first to go out of business. Stations selling premium at the lowest possible octane level were expected

---

[16]Convenient locations and smoothly functioning pumps are examples of services even low-service gas stations still provided. In general, if under competition a station was selling gasoline at a price higher than what it had paid for it (including transportation), some service must have been provided.

to be similarly affected. These implications are testable, although the data for the latter implication may be more difficult to collect than those for the former implication.

Gas station owners were able to alter still other margins of their product without violating the letter of the regulation. One of these margins was station hours. Station owners could choose their hours of operation, thereby lowering costs without violating the regulation. Selling gasoline in the middle of the night is more costly than during business hours because workers must be paid a higher wage to work at night and because security is more problematic. Perhaps because complex pricing schemes are costly to operate, twenty-four–hour stations charge the same price at all hours. The average cost of twenty-four–hour stations is higher than that of stations open only in daytime hours, and therefore the single price charged by the former must be higher than that charged by the latter. Price controls required stations to retain the old price but did not require them to keep the old hours. Most stations that had been open twenty-four hours a day quickly shortened their hours of service. Such stations were thus able to charge prices higher than those charged by others while incurring the same costs.[17]

Thus far I have considered only the margins of adjustment open to sellers. There also were margins at which buyers alone or buyers and sellers together could adjust in order to minimize dissipation. Resources spent in the queue were not received by others, and the existence of queues indicated that potential gains from sidestepping queues existed. One common way to circumvent price controls, and thus to lower the losses therefrom, was to tie the sale of gasoline to the sale of another product, not subject to price controls. Owners were able to use lubrication and other gas station services to mask the true price of gasoline to the regulators. A customer whose waiting cost for a full tank of gasoline was $5 was willing to pay up to $5 above the competitive price of lubrication when it was bundled up with a full tank of gas and no waiting. The seller who provided such bundles was able to capture some of the value that had formerly been dissipated by waiting. At no previous time in history had automobiles been so well lubricated.

THE MINIMIZATION OF DISSIPATION

It is useful here to return to the analysis of adjustment by sellers regarding customer service in order to bring out an important point developed by Cheung. In his analysis of price controls Cheung recognizes that the initial attenuation of the property rights structure would put some potential

---

[17]Eventually, most stations reduced their hours to the minimum (and most convenient to them) required to dispense their gasoline allocation.

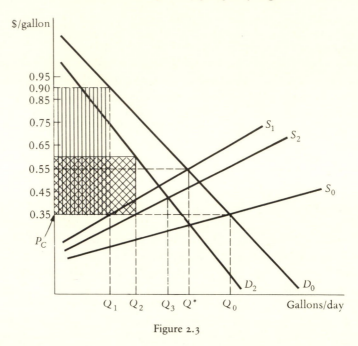

Figure 2.3

income in the public domain, thus leading to income dissipation to the extent that resources were spent to capture the non-exclusive income. An equally important point made by Cheung is that the maximization hypothesis implies that all such dissipation will be a constrained minimum. Dissipation is simply the process of adjusting to new constraints – here the constraint is price controls. By adjusting their levels of service downward as the constraint of price controls became binding, sellers were able to capture value that would otherwise have been left in the public domain. This action is a component of the minimization of dissipation.

Consider the following example, depicted in Figure 2.3. S_0 and D_0 represent the market conditions for full-service regular gasoline before the supply decrease and before the implementation of price controls, and P_C, 35 cents per gallon, represents the market price. That price ultimately became the control price. When the supply shifted, S_1 representing the new supply, price controls became binding. Had sellers continued to offer full service, they would have supplied a quantity Q_1 for which consumers were willing to pay 90 cents per gallon. The difference between that price and the control price, 55 cents per gallon, would have been dissipated in the form of time spent in the queue. The total value of the queuing dissipation is shown by the shaded rectangle. This 55 cents per gallon was lost in the sense that the customer's time expenditure was received by no one. As indicated, the (maximizing) seller could capture some of this dissipated income by reducing gasoline quality and gasoline services.

Because gasoline continued to be sold by the gallon, the coordinates of Figure 2.3 have the right units for the changed product, but the supply and demand curves for the new quality must be redrawn. S_2 is the new supply of gasoline, which required fewer resources because of the elimination of services. Consumers' valuation of the no-service gasoline was less than that of full-service gasoline; the new demand is shown by D_2. The services eliminated, however, were valued by consumers more than they cost to produce; this is why they were provided to begin with. Therefore, the intersection between S_2 and D_2 (at quantity Q_3), the no-service curves, must then be to the left of the intersection between D_0 and S_1 at quantity Q^*. This is a reflection of a cost of regulation that the adjustments could not eliminate. The dissipation per gallon was reduced (to near 25 cents in the example), and the number of gallons of gasoline (Q_2) was larger than in the absence of the adjustment (Q_1). The total dissipation, after service reduction, is shown by the hatched area and (combined with the appropriate "welfare triangles") is less than the dissipation without the service reduction.[18]

Before October 1973, the adjustment in gasoline quality was sufficient to yield an equilibrium price as low as 35 cents per gallon, and thus no waiting lines emerged. After October 1973, the price control constraint in the gasoline market was so severe that even when all the available adjustments had been taken advantage of, the equilibrium price exceeded 35 cents a gallon. Consequently, shortages ensued and queues were required to ration the available quantity.

CONCLUSION

Analysis of rationing by waiting and of price controls brings out the fact that because of the complexity of transactions, market participants have many margins besides quantity and price to which they can adjust. Maximization implies that such margins will be exploited, and the pattern of that exploitation is predictable: People will use the lowest-cost methods available to them under the constraints to reclaim the value that the regulations place in the public domain. As a result of such actions, dissipation from the regulations is minimized. In the case of the 1970s gasoline price controls, the adjustments took form as the lowest permitted gasoline octane levels, the shortest possible hours of operation for service stations, and the very frequent lubrication of automobiles.

[18]The service reduction also reduced the magnitude of the shortage induced by price controls. Before the service reduction, the shortage is ($Q_0 - Q_1$). After the service reduction, the shortage falls.

3

The costs of contracting: the tenancy contract

The study of contracts lies at the heart of the study of property rights. Contracts, whether formal or informal, reallocate rights among contracting parties; the tenancy contract between tenant and landlord – between the owner of labor and the owner of land – is relatively simple and is thus appropriate to the commencement of the study of contracts.

On a family farm a single operator or a single family – the owner of labor – undertakes the bulk of farm activities. Family farming is common and relatively simply organized. By studying tenancy contracts in the context of family farming, it is possible to isolate some basic contracting problems that may be obscured in more complex organizations. As a background to the analysis of the tenancy contract I offer a critical review of the traditional approach to the relationship between tenant and landlord.

THE STUDY OF THE SHARE CONTRACT, AND CHEUNG'S CONTRIBUTION TO IT

Price theory textbooks routinely introduce the notion of a production function and discuss the marginal product of a factor such as labor for given levels of such other factors as capital and land. Given the productivity of the factors and the market prices of factors and products, it is easy to determine both the optimum amounts and the values of the contributions of each factor. The assumptions that factors are uniform and that all relevant information is freely available usually underlie such discussions. In such a setting, the problem of organizing production is trivial.

These textbook assumptions are violated in reality. In agriculture, weather, pests, and other forces affect output differently in different periods and in different locations. In addition, no two pieces of land or two workers are identical to each other. Determining the properties of each unit of input requires extensive and costly measurement. Owing to diversity in the forces that affect output, the specific contributions of individuals are extremely difficult to determine. Individuals, therefore, can mask their own low-level contributions by attributing them to other forces. Such attempts to capture wealth make cooperation among individuals costly, and, as will be shown, individuals can gain by organizing their transactions in ways that lower these costs.

The inefficiency associated with the share contract is a particular manifestation of the wealth-capture problem that was recognized long ago and that has received a great deal of attention from economists. In a share contract, a landlord lets a tenant work the land for a share of the output. The tenant's pay to the landlord appears to be similar to an ad valorem tax, and this analogy has been used to suggest that the share contract is inefficient.

Consider first, briefly, the ad valorem tax. The demand facing sellers of a taxed commodity is lower than the consumers' demand by the amount of the tax. Because of the shift in demand, the market equilibrium quantity under the tax is less than it is in the absence of the tax. The tax, then, distorts resource allocation: Under the tax, the marginal unit is valued at more than it costs; expanding production would produce a net gain, but the tax creates a wedge that prevents the realization of that gain.

Economists have argued that this tax analysis applies directly to the share contract. In Figure 3.1, adapted from Cheung (1969, p. 43), the tenant's marginal product on a plot of a given size is M_{PL}, and her or his market wage is W. Were the tenant self-employed, she or he would apply L^* units of time to the farm. The landlord, however, receives a share of the output. The tenant whose share of the output is $(1 - r)$ then retains only $(1 - r)$ of her or his own marginal product, and in order to maximize wealth she or he will apply L^T units of time to the farm. For units of labor between L^T and L^*, the output value of the tenant exceeds the wage rate, but the tenant will prefer to sell these units of labor service in the market, because, per unit of labor, her or his share in the farm output is less than W. Such tenants, then, will stop short of producing the output at which the value of their marginal product equals their alternative earning. The shaded area in Figure 3.1 is the alleged inefficiency induced by the share contract and is comparable to the tax distortion.

The tax analogy contains two implicit, and by no means innocent, assumptions. One is that landlords find it prohibitively expensive to stipulate and police the amount of labor input; the other is that landlords encounter no cost in policing the receipt of their share of the output. Whereas either assumption may be a good approximation of real circumstances in any particular case, the two are unlikely to hold true simultaneously. The assumptions that the cost of monitoring output is always zero and that the cost of monitoring labor input is always prohibitive, implicit in the traditional approach to the share contract, are ad hoc.

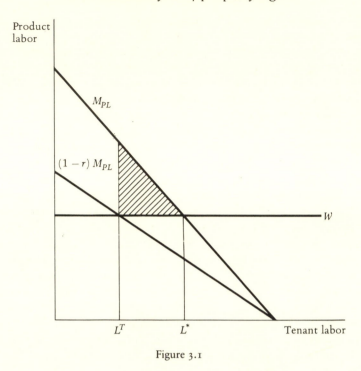

Figure 3.1

In his ground-breaking work on the theory of share tenancy, which he tested empirically against observed practices in China, Cheung (1969) makes several points that are pertinent to the discussion here. The first, consistent with the Coase Theorem, is that in a world of zero transactions costs, the share contract will yield an efficient outcome, as will other contract forms. This is because contractors can costlessly add and police contract stipulations in such a way that all inefficiency is eliminated. Second, Cheung points out that sharecropping is unlikely to have been inefficient, given its long history of survival. Third, he spells out some of the stipulations that were necessary for efficiency to have been attained in sharecropping. Among these are fixed plot size, required levels of other inputs, and restrictions on allowed crops. Finding that practices in China were consistent with these implications, Cheung proceeds to argue that risk aversion may explain the prevalence of share tenancy, because under share tenancy the landlord and the tenant share in the vagaries of variations in output and in output value. Whereas Cheung's critique of the received analysis that claims that the share contract distorts the allocation of resources is well taken, his risk-aversion explanation is not.

Risk aversion does not satisfactorily explain the share contract. Attitude toward risk is a matter of taste. If, as we usually assume, taste is a personal matter that may vary unpredictably across individuals, an explanation based on risk aversion is not refutable. Even the assumption of uniformity of tastes toward risk, that is, the making of risk aversion a function of such observable variables as wealth, is still not sufficient to explain sharecropping. In a zero transaction cost world, sharecropping by itself is not an attractive method of sharing risk. Share contracting does distribute the crop of a single plot between the two parties, but there are other ways to distribute variability that can remove more of the risk. For instance, because two persons residing on opposite sides of the globe are not subject to common random forces, pooling the risks between them reduces the risk each would face alone. Under the assumption of costless transactions, such pooling involves no added costs and thus will be practiced. In reality, of course, transacting is costly, rendering some risk pooling difficult to effect. When transacting is costly, however, all contract forms are costly; and in that case sharing may be chosen not, or at least not only, for its effect on risk but also because of some properties of transaction costs. Moreover, when transacting is costly, other contracts may be chosen in spite of their riskiness. Next I offer a transaction cost hypothesis to explain sharing; in subsequent chapters I offer transaction cost hypotheses to explain other forms of organization, assuming throughout that people are risk-neutral.[1]

THREE METHODS OF COLLABORATION BETWEEN OWNERS OF LAND AND OWNERS OF LABOR

Given the total amounts of land and labor, there is some plot size or, more generally, some size distribution of plots that maximizes total output. Only a fraction of workers, however, own the commensurate amount of land. Those who own more land than they can most profitably cultivate by themselves can gain by cooperating with those whose holdings are too small. In order to realize the gains, the factor owners must contract with each other. I consider here three methods by which two owners can collaborate and in which ownership patterns are preserved: (1) the wage contract, (2) the rental contract, and (3) the share contract. The discussion of the consolidation of ownership will follow.

It was pointed out earlier that individual specimens of both land and

[1]When the sole contractual problem between tenant and landlord is the method of dividing output, the role of risk aversion seems both simple and important. If, however, many sources of variability confront the parties, the role of risk aversion in contracting for the assignment of any of such sources becomes much less clear and much less important. For instance, it is not at all clear how transferring the maintenance of irrigation ditches from the landlord to the tenant affects the distribution of risk.

labor are not uniform, and that, in addition, production is subject to variability due to factors such as weather and pests. Output, therefore, will vary from plot to plot not only because of the variability in both of the inputs but also because of random variability. Characteristics of the variability are crucial to the choice among contracts.

Before analyzing the general case in which both land and labor are variable, I will consider the special cases in which either the land or the labor is uniform. Suppose that land is entirely uniform and unchangeable. If collaboration is by a wage contract, workers can gain by shirking, exerting themselves less than they would were they self-employed. Because output is subject to variability both because of random factors affecting output directly and because workers' contributions to output vary, it is difficult to isolate the effect of change in effort from the effect of the random factors. Workers, of course, will be supervised, but given that supervision is costly and subject to economy, workers will not be fully penalized for a reduction in effort, and such a reduction is therefore expected. Wage payment is accordingly adjusted to the expected reduction in effort, and workers' real income ultimately declines as a result of shirking. Lowering the wage implies that shirking in penalized; workers are paid, on average, for what work they accomplish. Such workers would prefer to work harder and be paid more, because they operate at a point at which the cost to them of an extra unit of effort is less than the corresponding value of the increase in output brought about by that effort; but the cost of effecting such an arrangement exceeds the gain it would generate. Under the given conditions, then, the wage contract requires costly supervision, and labor is not applied at the rate that self-employed workers would choose.

Tenants who operate under share contracts retain a portion, but not all, of their marginal product. Although the incentive to shirk is not as strong here as it is in the wage contract, it is induced by the same factors, and the preceding discussion of the wage contract applies.

Tenants who collaborate with landowners by renting their land pay a fixed amount for its use. Output will differ from that expected, first, because of random fluctuations, and, second, to the extent that the tenants alter their own effort. Since land is uniform, land does not contribute to output variability; the tenants' expected output, then, varies only as a function of their own effort. The tenant is the "residual claimant"; barring bankruptcy, the landlord receives a fixed amount, and the tenant receives whatever is left over after paying the rent (this difference may, of course, be a negative amount). Apart from the random element, tenants' reward is strictly a function of their own effort.[2]

---

[2] The fact that the fixed-rent contract has not been claimed to be inefficient suggests that land (inclusive of the improvement and equipment that accompanied it) has been viewed as unchangeable. On the other hand, economists have been quick to criticize

The analysis of the situation where land is heterogeneous and labor (and labor effort) uniform is the mirror image of the one presented above. When labor is uniform, wage contracts make expected output a function of the quality of the land only. Landlords, then, have the right incentive to maintain and improve their land and will not gain from misrepresenting its quality. In this case, the landlords are the residual claimants, and they are the only ones affected by their own actions. A rental (or a share) contract would be inefficient here, producing less total income for the contracting parties. The more efficient contract, that of the fixed wage, would prevail under such conditions.

But neither land nor labor is generally uniform. All three contract forms are, then, subject to efficiency problems. When discrepancies between costs and valuations are inevitable, an arrangement in which such problems are observed cannot be thought of as inefficient. Inefficiency implies preventable waste – that would not occur if people were to maximize. In an imperfect world, even the best solution is still subject to discrepancies between marginal costs and marginal valuations, because not all such discrepancies can be eliminated economically. There is no point, then, in investigators' attempts to discover inefficiencies, that is, situations that can be improved upon, because these are not discoverable given the assumption of maximization. Our task is, rather, to determine what changes in resource allocation and in economic organization will be brought about by a change in circumstances. In order to be able to analyze changes in resource allocation, a more detailed discussion of the nature of variability is necessary.

THE EFFECTS OF VARIABILITY WITHIN FACTORS

Because it is commonly, though only implicitly, assumed that land is uniform and unchangeable it is instructive to probe into the nature of land and the effects of variability in it. Each acre of land differs from all others, even from the ones adjacent to it, in a variety of ways: in the incidence of rocks, in steepness, in the degree of soil erosion, in the amounts of various nutrients, in exposure to the wind and sun. Land parcels also differ from one another in such features as access to groundwater, quality and quantity of irrigation canals, availability of pumping equipment, types of roads serving them, and distance to markets. Moreover, the ease of exploiting such features also varies. Land use

Henry George's single-tax proposal, pointing out that since his assumption that land was unchangeable was too far from reality, his policy conclusions were rendered useless. Had economists been consistent in recognizing in all their applications that land is changeable, it is less likely that the share contract would have been singled out as the only inefficient tenure contract: The fixed-rent contract would also have been considered inefficient.

would be efficient if landlords were compensated by users of land for the exact reduction in land value. Because land is not uniform, however, the exact evaluation of these effects requires measurement at every spot. Exact and comprehensive measurements are obviously prohibitively costly, and thus measurements are neither exact nor comprehensive. Indeed, certain features may not be measured at all.

Tenants who can gain from exploiting those land attributes that they are not marginally charged for will use them to the point at which the net gain they yield falls to zero. Thus, even though there are only two parties to the transaction, an unpriced attribute is effectively placed in the public domain. Tenants can capture such an attribute by simply exploiting it; capture is costly to the transactors because exploitation is carried beyond the point where the value of its contribution equals the reduction in its value and where the value of the land declines more than the value of output increases.

Any land attribute that can be changed by the tenant and is not charged for by the landlord becomes a free attribute to the tenant and is then subject to overuse. Similarly, any changeable land attribute that remains under the landlord's control will be undersupplied. If the landlord is not contractually committed to maintaining capital improvements, she or he is likely to postpone doing so beyond the contract period. All such inefficient practices reduce joint wealth and ultimately harm the two parties, inducing both to seek methods to lower such inefficiences and to maximize the net value of their resources.

METHODS FOR RESTRAINING LOSSES

Labor and land are complex factors, each with many attributes, but contracts between pairs of owners are usually quite simple. How are the individual attributes, then, controlled by contract, and what forces determine which contract will maximize the value of the resources? A fixed-rent land contract can simply stipulate duration and rent; alternatively, it can be as detailed as the contracting parties wish it to be.[3] Whereas contractors are free to stipulate whatever they wish, not all attributes are worth stipulating and monitoring. Any attribute that is not stipulated and that can be varied becomes a free attribute. Tenants who are in control of such an attribute will use extra units so long as they generate added positive (net) income; landlords will similarly use attributes under their control.

Although by assumption the loss associated with free attributes is too

[3]In either case, a mechanism to enforce contract performance is required. Such a mechanism is usually provided partly by the contractors and partly by the courts. The existence of such a mechanism will be taken here as a given.

costly to avert directly, it can be controlled in two distinct general ways: by altering contract stipulations regarding attributes related to the ones subject to excessive exploitation or inadequate provision, or by switching to an altogether different contract that directly controls those attributes left uncontrolled under the first contract.

Manipulating related attributes

The tenancy contract involves many attributes that are costly to stipulate. Similarly, the parties can affect many dimensions of their transaction in order to maximize the value of their exchange and lower dissipation. They can manipulate prices of commodities related to hard-to-control attributes, manipulate corresponding quantities, and manipulate contract duration.

The excessive use of free attributes may be controlled by exploiting the fact that the consumption of a commodity will change when the prices or quantities of related commodities change. In the case of a soil nutrient, for instance, the difficulty in measuring its use over the rental area pre-cludes its direct pricing and turns it into a free attribute. Its use, however, may be curbed by the appropriate manipulation of substitute or comple-mentary attributes – for example, lowering the price of a substitute. If a landlord lowers the price his tenant pays for a fertilizer that is a substitute for the soil nutrient, the tenant's demand for, and level of use of, the nutrient will fall. It is true that the price subsidy will result in excessive use of the fertilizer; however, there is always a subsidized price for the substitute commodity that generates a combined net gain.

One cost of effecting such a subsidy is the need to fine-tune it: When-ever conditions change, its level must be calculated anew. A particular low-transaction-cost application of a price subsidy is to provide free of charge whatever amount of the fertilizer the tenant wishes to use. The tenant's incentive to overuse the fertilizer as well as to sell it correspond-ingly increases. Nevertheless, in some cases the added cost will still be less than the loss reduction in conserving the soil nutrient.[4] A nutrient-control method that is closely related to that of a price subsidy and that may be employed by the landlord is the provision of a fixed quantity of the fertilizer at no charge. It will, like the method above, lower the demand for and the use of the soil nutrient.

Duration is another contract feature that affects the parties' behavior with regard to attributes. A wheatland owner may find a one-year rental contract satisfactory. On the other hand, in the case of an orchard, the

---

[4] A price subsidy (and other practices to be described) will be effective only if the cost of reselling it exceeds the tenant's gain from using it. One particular transaction cost permits reducing the loss from another.

care and maintenance of the trees, which can be most efficiently provided by the tenant, become free attributes to a one-year tenant, whereas a longer-term rental contract enhances the tenant's incentive for care and maintenance, thus reducing the tenant's exploitation of these attributes.

The task of caring for the trees need not be assigned to the tenant, just as equipment maintenance is not necessarily a tenant's task. Such assignments are a matter of choice: The contractors are expected to assign the provision of particular attributes to whichever party is more suitable. The existence of such a choice points to another aspect of the loss-restraining problem. It may seem that in the land-rent contract it is clear which inputs each contractor furnishes: The landowner supplies the land and the tenant the labor. The recognition, however, that any commodity is a collection of attributes suggests that the real situation is more complex. Improvements, for instance, are obviously not an integral part of the land, and the contractors are free to decide which party will take charge of any of them.[5] More generally, the contractors have leeway in deciding which of them should furnish particular attributes.

With regard to each attribute, one can ask: Which of the two parties will be more inclined than the other to affect the (net) value of output by manipulating that attribute? The principle I applied earlier to labor and land applies also to individual attributes. If the party that will be more inclined to affect the outcome by varying the level of an attribute is put in control of that attribute, becoming, therefore, the residual claimant of its variability, misallocation will be minimized. If, for example, land is rented out on an annual basis, the maintenance of long-lasting improvements will tend to be placed in the landlords' charge, because they are the chief beneficiaries of proper maintenance through the higher rents they can charge for future periods.

Changing the contract form

In the preceding section it was shown that the fixed-rent contract places various land attributes in the public domain and that the associated losses can be lowered by manipulating the prices and quantities of related goods. The overuse of those various contract atttributes that are not directly controlled may be curbed, then; however, it cannot be eliminated. It is proper to ask whether collaboration between owners of land

---

[5]If landlords are legally required to keep certain improvements present on the plot at the time the contract is signed, there is no need to spell this out in the contract. Similarly, if a landlord plans to maintain the improvements, she or he will not require such maintenance from the tenant. Some contracts, then, may appear to be lacking in detail but, nevertheless, may differ significantly from similarly worded tenancy contracts in areas where the particular improvements are simply absent.

and owners of labor should occur through a contract that is an alternative to the land-rent contract.

Any contract is subject to problems of non-optimal use, and therefore no single contract is best under all circumstances. Changes in the circumstances that affect contract choice may be gradual, but the change in contract *form* cannot be gradual; either it takes place or it does not. Thus, a comparison between contract forms must be "global"; total net values must be calculated in order to determine which contract generates the highest net gain. Economists are not equipped to make such comparisons directly. Conditions under which a switch from one form to another is likely, however, can be spelled out. Turning to the three contract forms here, one refutable implication of the model above is that when market wage rises relative to land rent, the contract form will shift away from the wage contract, which induces (relatively) careless use of labor, to the land-rent contract (though perhaps first to the share contract), which induces relatively careless use of land. In order to be able to compare the different contract forms, however, we should first study share contracting.

ADVANTAGES AND DISADVANTAGES OF SHARING

The share tenancy contract stands halfway between the fixed-rent and the wage contract. When sharing, both the landowner and the tenant are residual claimants, because each is remunerated by a fraction of whatever the output is. At the same time, each gains from shirking; the landowner will not maintain land improvements as vigorously as she or he would under the wage contract, and the tenant will not work as hard as she or he would under the fixed-rent contract. The margins subject to distortion under the share contract include, then, all those of the other two contracts. In addition, the specification and monitoring of output are likely to consume more resources under the share contract than under the other contract forms. Although more margins are subject to distortion when the contract calls for sharing, the loss from each margin of distortion is reduced more than proportionately. A new angle on the previously discussed tax analogy may demonstrate how the share contract can result in a lower level of distortions than the level associated with the other two contracts.

The analysis of tax distortions is standard fare in taxation literature. It is well known that the distortion associated with a tax (or with a subsidy) rises as the square of the tax (or subsidy) rate. Thus the welfare-loss triangle of a 10 percent tax on a commodity is (approximately) four times as large as that of a 5 percent tax on the same commodity. In the wage contract, the reduction in effort is a free attribute available to the worker, because the worker is not penalized for the reduced effort; it is as if the worker were to pay a 100 percent tax on the increase in output induced by greater effort. Similarly, under the fixed-rent contract, it is as if the tenant were to receive a 100 percent subsidy on soil nutrients and the landlord were to pay a 100 percent tax on land improvements yielding returns within the contract period. In a share contract, these taxes and subsidies are reduced from 100 percent to the worker's share in the case of the extra effort; the subsidies are similarly reduced in the case of the soil nutrient, and a tax of 100 percent is reduced to the landlord's share in the case of the maintenance expenses. A fifty–fifty sharing arrangement would reduce the distortions from each of the attributes to one-fourth of their levels at the 100 percent tax or subsidy. Whereas *all* of these items are taxed or subsidized in a share contract, compared with only about *half* of them being taxed or subsidized when one or the other of the two contract forms is used, the quadratic relationship is capable of lessening the total burden under the share contract to a level below that of the burden either of the other forms generates. The share contract, however, entails an increase in monitoring costs, which may tip the scale against it.

Monitoring serves to reduce the losses associated with margins of distortion. The monitoring of each margin of distortion, however, entails its own start-up cost. Since the share contract is subject to more margins of distortion than are the other two contracts, its costs of monitoring are higher. The gains the share contract is capable of generating in reduced distortions, then, may not be large enough, and the share contract may fail to be adopted. As conditions gradually shift, favoring, say, the wage contract over the fixed-rent contract, the share contract becomes attractive as an intermediate step; nevertheless, because of the extra monitoring costs required, the share contract may be skipped completely.[6] As the fixed-rent contract becomes less attractive, the fraction of rent contracts is expected to fall and the fraction of wage contracts is expected to increase; but it is not possible to state, a priori, whether the fraction of share contracts will increase or fall. Besides the three contract forms emphasized here, there is one other arrangement that merits special attention: sole ownership.

COSTS OF SOLE OWNERSHIP

I have focused so far on the costs and gains associated with fixed wages, fixed rents, and share contracts between owners of land and of labor. Although different contracts encounter different incentive problems, every exchange, and therefore every contract, is subject to some such problems. The sole-ownership arrangement is free of those contracting problems that arise when land and labor are not owned by the same individual; it may

[6]Not only is a fifty–fifty sharing formula simpler to administer than others, it also tends to yield the highest reduction in distortions. As the value of the contributions of the two parties become more equal, a sharing arrangement is more likely to emerge.

seem, then, that sole ownership should be the preferred method of operation. The sole-ownership arrangement, however, is subject to two sets of transaction costs associated with owning all of the inputs in a production process. The first set of costs arises because the pattern of ownership of productive non-human assets is extremely unlikely to match fully the ownership pattern of human skills that would have generated the highest output. Total output, then, can be increased if people exchange productive assets in order to arrive at a better match of resources. To accomplish this, owners of labor would have to borrow in order to buy the land with which to work. This would not occur unless transacting is reintroduced – here the transaction between borrower and lender replacing that between owner of labor and owner of land – and it cannot be determined a priori that the transaction between the former two would yield a higher net gain than the transaction between the latter two.

The second, and equally important, set of costs of sole ownership is due to the losses in specialization that occur when one individual owns and uses all of the productive inputs. Although sole ownership does remove the incentive to shirk, the gains from specialization are also forgone. In order to maximize the return from their land, landowners will engage in such activities as maintenance work and prevention of erosion. The owners of labor will invest in such activities as maintaining and improving their cultivation skills. A person who owns both assets cannot profitably specialize as much as the two individual owners of the two assets can. Moreover, the notion that land and labor can produce output is a gross oversimplification; the output is produced by numerous production factors. Farmers are seldom, if ever, the sole owners of all inputs. A true contemporary sole-owner farmer in the United States would, among other things, have to own and operate her or his own spray plane and conduct her or his own plant research and development. As markets grow larger, the potential gains from specialization should increase, and any one individual should gain from relinquishing ownership of various assets (or attributes of some asset) and engaging in contracting with owners of other inputs in order to acquire the corresponding services. The gains from sole ownership must, then, be balanced against the falling output caused by the commensurate lower level of specializing.

SOME IMPLICATIONS

The contracting model discussed thus far can generate many implications with regard to actual tenancy practices. Because information problems are at the heart of the high cost of transacting, I will concentrate on those implications that are a direct consequence of information problems. Two sources of change in information costs will be considered, one associated with the introduction of a new crop, the other with the arrival of new workers.

When a crop new to an area becomes profitable, information on how well it will do in different locations within the area is more costly to obtain than is similar information on old crops. Landowners who personally cultivate only part of their holdings and contract with others to cultivate the rest of their land know, as a rule, more about their land than do their tenants. Because they are also the main beneficiaries of good decisions about new crops, the discrepancy in landlord versus tenant knowledge for the new crop is likely to be higher than it was for the old crop. Tenants who are offered fixed-rent contracts may suspect that the rent landlords demand is excessive and that the landlords are exaggerating their plots' productiveness in growing the new crop. Such suspicion is hard to allay, and so the tenants' demand for land and their associated counteroffers are likely to be low. Wage contracts are free of this particular problem because landlords who pay fixed wages bear the entire new-crop risk, about which they are better informed than are the tenants. As more landowners switch to the new crop, wage contracts should become more common. In addition, it is expected that, as time passes, the trend will be reversed, at least in part; with time, the cost of determining the suitability of land parcels to the new crop will decline, inducing the readoption of fixed-rent contracts where they were preferred before.

Another information problem arises with immigration. Little is known about how workers who are new to an area will perform. Landowners are reluctant to commit themselves to paying new workers the prevailing wage. Given the lack of knowledge regarding workers' abilities and attitudes, both demand for the services of such workers and, consequently, the wage offered are likely to be low. A new worker who believes that she or he is more productive than the wage she or he is offered indicates can "guarantee" her or his output by offering to operate as a fixed-rent tenant. The worker, then, bears the onus of the information problem. Therefore, it is expected that relatively more new workers than established ones will operate as fixed-rent tenants. Moreover, new tenants will be given parcels that are less easy to exploit, such as those containing few improvements. Some old-time tenants may acquire a reputation for being gentle on the land and on improvements; these individuals will be favored. Newcomers do not have such reputations and are therefore expected to get land parcels for which the lack of information makes less difference.

CONCLUSIONS

The owners of labor and of land can increase the value of their assets by collaborating, because total output is then larger than it would be were

Source of losses from various contractual forms

	Policing labor	Policing land	Policing output	Lack of specializing
High losses	FW	FR	SC	SO
Intermediate losses	SC	SC	FW, FR	SC
Low or no losses	FR, SO	FW, SO	SO	FW, FR

SO: Sole owner of land and labor
SC: Share contract
FW: Fixed-wage contract
FR: Fixed-rent contract

they to operate alone. Effecting the collaboration, however, is itself costly because it is difficult to prevent wealth capture when cooperation is attempted. Measuring each factor's contribution to output is necessary for successful cooperation. Such measurements are costly and therefore will not be precise. This lack of precision, coupled with the variability in output due to unpredictable factors such as the weather, implies that individuals can gain at each other's expense and that they will spend resources in order to capture these gains. Together, owners of labor and owners of land (bolstered by competition from other owners) will adopt the contract form that generates the largest net output value where maximization is subject to conventional production costs as well as to the costs associated with the capture of wealth.

Neither labor nor land is uniform; specimens of each vary in the levels of their different attributes. The contract between the owners, therefore, will attempt to control not only the factors as a whole but also various individual attributes. Some of these attributes may be controlled directly (e.g., a tenant pays for irrigation water supplied by the landlord); ones that are difficult to control directly may be controlled indirectly by fixing quantities and altering prices. A basic principle underlying the maximization process is that individual attributes will be placed under the control of the party who can more readily affect the net value of the outcome by manipulating the attribute.

The accompanying table catalogues and compares the losses associated with the various contractual arrangements analyzed in this chapter. This table brings out most clearly that no one solution is best under all circumstances. As circumstances change, the form of organization will tend to change, too.

4

The old firm and the new organization

For a long time the theory of economic organization and the theory of the firm were nearly synonymous. Standard economics textbooks occasionally referred to other forms of organization, such as the family and government; but the firm was the only organization consistently and systematically discussed. Nevertheless, the exact function of the firm remained unclear. Knight's (1921) attempt to add substance to the construct called "the firm" did not fare very well, and Coase's (1937) revolutionary approach to organization required several decades as well as his own work on social cost to begin to influence economists. Both of these efforts focused on the firm. In more recent decades, Coase's transaction cost ideas have been exploited both by economists attempting to generate a theory of the firm and by others questioning the usefulness of such a theory.[1] The insights gained through these efforts have been considerable; nevertheless our understanding of organization is still only in its infancy. In this chapter, the transaction cost approach to organization is extended.

Different subsets of attributes of assets possessing many attributes tend to be owned by different individuals. Explaining the pattern of such ownership is central to the study of organization. My thesis in this extension is that as a transactor's ability to affect the outcome of an aspect of a transaction increases, the transactor will assume more responsibility for the associated variability; that is, she or he will tend to assume a greater share of, and thus become more of a residual claimant to, the income of attributes she or he can affect. Consequently, the ownership of physical entities may be divided, enabling the owners (and the users) of different attributes to be separate individuals. The management of entities with divided ownership requires "organization," the subject of this chapter. In

[1] Prominent among these are Alchian and Demsetz (1972), Williamson (1975), Jensen and Meckling (1976), Klein, Crawford, and Alchian (1978), and Cheung (1983).

42

order to appreciate the need for the transaction cost approach and its contribution, the received model of the firm must first be assessed. I will attempt to show that as a description of real firms the received model of the firm is untenable, and that under conditions that would allow a textbook firm to exist its function would become inconsequential.

A CRITIQUE OF THE RECEIVED MODEL OF THE FIRM

Underlying the received model of the firm is the production function: a relationship tracking the highest output any set of inputs can produce with the available technology. Returns to scale are assumed first to increase and ultimately to decline because of factors such as the uniqueness of specialized resources and the indivisibility of equipment and of organizers. The firm is simply an organization that selects (the optimal) points on the production function, acquires the necessary inputs, transforms them according to the production function into output, and sells that output. Its objective is profit maximization: basically, maximizing the difference between revenues and expenses. The cost function plays a major role in shaping the firm; of particular interest is the minimum point on the average cost function that determines the scale of the competitive firm.[2]

A major implicit assumption behind the conventional derivations is that of costless information, particularly of the production function itself and of the prices and the attributes of inputs and outputs. If information is freely available, then factors' contributions can be easily assessed, and monitoring their performance becomes superfluous. It is not surprising, then, that monitoring receives almost no attention in these discussions. Still, given human nature and the social character of production, even the notion of the production function itself poses some problems. This function may be a strictly technological relationship; however, as labor is one of the factors used in production, the question of how labor is actually applied is relevant. If points on the production function are to yield the highest output from given inputs, the labor input must be strained to the limit, which implies, for instance, that workers hired for a day should be exhausted by the end of the day. It is clear that workers seldom work to exhaustion; to a worker, effort is a variable under her or his control. The

[2]Duality theory relates costs and production functions. The emerging correspondence between the firm's cost functions and the production function, however, is treated at least some of the time as a definitional relationship. Varian (1984), for instance, discusses technology in some detail (pp. 8–20), in the process mentioning the firm several times without defining it; then, in the opening sentence of the section "The Competitive Firm," he states, "Now that we have considered ways to describe a firm's technological possibilities, we can begin to discuss its economic behavior" (p. 21). The firm, then, is *defined* in terms of the production function, and duality turns out to be a definitional rather than a functional relation.

supplier of labor, then, must decide on the desired level of effort and must communicate this information to the user of the labor services. Since the technological relationship has to be supplemented with human relations, production, particularly in its relation to cost, loses some of its technological innocence. More basic problems are encountered when one inquires into the contract form used in employing inputs and into the nature of the product.

What precisely does the firm produce? The implicit assumption employed in the standard approach seems to be that each firm performs only one function. It may seem that two firms generating the same output (the same Q) do indeed perform the same operations. In reality, however, most firms perform a large number of operations, and the operations performed by one are not always the same as those performed by the other. Consider wine as an output. Some wineries grow all the grapes they use to make wine, whereas others buy at least some of their grapes. It does not seem that such differences among firms are attributable to considerations of production function. Yet price theory texts uniformly seem to ignore the existence of such differences.[3] Stigler, for instance, states that "as parts of a large enterprise are decentralized, the gains of economies of scale are simultaneously sacrificed" (1966, p. 156). Decentralizing could be achieved without sacrificing scale economies if several vertical functions were performed initially. Because few firms perform only one function, it is hard to escape the conclusion that the textbook firm is presumed to produce whatever is necessary to make the textbook cost function constructs correct.[4]

One could argue that wine is not a sufficiently narrowly defined commodity and that the two wineries are actually producing different commodities. This, indeed, may be true. Similarly, Safeway and the corner grocery may be in different industries. Existing theory, however, does not provide a guide as to what constitutes different commodities. Any discrepancy across firms between the production and cost functions may, then, be attributed to differences in the commodities produced by such firms. The theory does not appear to be capable of refutation. In this light, it is not useful.

Specification of the precise units by which inputs are employed receives almost no attention in standard texts, yet in reality such units are diverse. In the case of labor, inputs are sometimes measured by time and sometimes by performance. Labor service is a major production function input

---

[3]Had traditional assessments of the firm routinely included raw materials among the inputs necessary to produce output, perhaps it would have been easier to recognize that the two wineries are different and, consequently, that the existence of such differences calls for some explanation.

[4]The spirit of my criticism of the received model is similar to Williamson's (1985).

that workers supply. The labor input the production function requires is in efficiency units: One worker contributing twice as many as another provides twice the labor input. In a similar vein, the demand for labor is taken as a function of labor's contribution to output. In the standard formulation of the cost function, however, labor when explicitly considered is not usually entered by units that correspond directly to its contribution.[5] Instead, the labor input entering the cost function is measured by the hour, and so labor is accounted for in units of time. Hours can readily substitute for efficiency units only if the relationships between the two are proportional. Because workers themselves are maximizers, it seems highly plausible that inducing workers to apply their time efficiently requires supervision. Moreover, supervision costs are unlikely to be proportional to labor costs; the relationship between the two is not likely to remain constant under all circumstances.

The use of the hour as the unit of labor input in cost functions, then, is not justified by standard production function considerations, and it is improper to switch from one function to the other unless account is taken of information and supervision problems. The reason hours are nevertheless used in cost functions seems to be simply that the dominant mode of employing labor happens to be by time, and the assumption of proportionality between actual hours and efficiency units is made in order that hours may be employed in production function analyses.[6]

The need for supervision arises because the factors contributing to a firm's production are not all owned by the same person. The ownership of factors used by the firm, however, is seldom explored in the received analysis, even though the typical implicit ownership assumptions are not innocuous. Firms are assumed to own the capital equipment they use and to hire labor. Hiring labor means renting laborers from the owners of the capital good "labor." In a non-slave economy, workers allow firms to use some of the services the capital good can generate. If firms choose to own their capital equipment rather than rent it, then rental is more problematic than ownership; it is plausible, then, that the use of labor, too, is problematic. In reality, not all capital used by firms is owned by them; capital is also rented in part. First, to the extent that firms are financed by borrowing, they are renting rather than owning the capital; and second, firms often rent space and equipment. It is not self-evident that those firm owners who borrow or rent capital and who employ labor have interests that coincide with the interests of the owners of the rented assets in how

[5]In some texts, particularly those viewed as advanced, the productive factors are introduced generically, with no recognition of institutional differences among factors.

[6]It is sometimes asserted that it is impossible to measure separately individuals' contributions to output. Under the given information assumptions, workers should, nevertheless, be rewarded for their effort and not for their time.

these assets should be employed. The question of whether these interests coincide is simply ignored, as a rule, in the textbook analysis of the firm. If asset owners' interests do not coincide, then methods of reconciling them must be considered.

Exploring a costless-transaction world may of course be appropriate for some analyses. It is not appropriate or useful, however, for analysis of the firm. Costless transacting dispenses with the problems of supervision and of divergence of interests among collaborating owners of assets. In the textbook characterization of firms, the inputs purchased in the market are assumed to perform the tasks expected of them automatically and fully. This would hold true if the relationship between inputs and outputs were costlessly observable, because then input owners could be remunerated strictly on the basis of their contributions; such costless observability is one of the features necessary (and indeed sufficient) for costless transacting to exist. Were transacting costless, the employer could, for instance, costlessly observe whether or not workers' time is perfectly utilized and could compensate workers accordingly. Under such conditions, however, any other method of remuneration could be as easily implemented. It does not matter, then, whether the nominal unit of pay is taken to be the wage, the contribution to output, or any other unit; each can be converted to any of the others without slippage. A firm, therefore, could function smoothly; but the market where direction is strictly by prices would perform just as smoothly. A model in which firms perform a nontrivial role must incorporate the costs of transacting.

It is by now a well-accepted idea that evaluating the contribution of a factor to output is costly, and that consequently such evaluations are not expected to be performed with complete accuracy. In the presence of inaccuracies, factor owners who rent out their assets for a given rate of pay will gain by reducing their effort. The transition from the production function to the cost function inevitably involves shirking under dispersed factor ownership. Maximizing individuals must take into account the effects of such shirking and must devise methods to lower the associated losses. Therefore, when the evaluation of performance is costly, the choice of contracts among cooperating factors becomes significant.

DIVIDED OWNERSHIP OF EQUIPMENT

Whereas I will show that the existence of scale economies in production is neither necessary nor sufficient for the existence of a large-scale organization, it is convenient to introduce positive transaction costs by considering problems associated with such a large scale. Large-scale economies can be attained by a centralizing organization, but the participating owners of resources have opportunities to shirk then. Alternatively, such economies may be attained by turning each resource owner into a residual claimant, but various attributes of the large-scale activity are then left in the public domain. I shall argue that the actual solutions to such problems are a mixture of the two forms of organization; that, as a rule, of the resource owners associated with the operation, several subsets become residual claimants to different components of the large-scale operation.

Among the factors that determine whether large-scale operations are advantageous are the management of an innovation, the research required for marketing, the pricing of a commodity, and the scale of equipment. A large-scale operation, however, does not as such necessarily require a large-scale organization. The most efficient equipment scale may require the work of several persons, but these need not all belong to the same organization; each may assume full control of her or his corner of the operation. Each may raise some capital, purchase other inputs, and sell output, thus becoming the residual claimant to her or his niche of the operation. Presumably, each individual would also have unrestricted access to "her" or "his" part of the equipment. A common-property problem may arise from this last condition.

I shall use three capital goods – a taxicab, a large machine, and an office building – to illustrate the nature of this problem. Problems with the use of the first two goods will be described only briefly; I shall use the third more extensively. These examples encompass the several problems encountered with equipment use and some of the different methods for resolving them.

A taxicab may be owned by two or more individuals who drive it in shifts. Various aspects of their operation such as wear and tear on tires and on upholstery are too costly to monitor and may become common property; since the individuals' shares of the damageable attributes are not fully separable, they are not well defined. When only two individuals share in the ownership of such an asset, the unpriced attribute will be consumed as if it were half free; in this way it becomes, in part, common property.[7] The ease of controlling the common-property problem is different for different attributes. For instance, the time slots allotted to each owner may be clearly delineated; the common-property problem in the use of gasoline depends on the accuracy of the fuel gauge; that of the tires depends on how easy it is to keep track of individuals' mileage – very easy – and to keep track of tire damage (think of type of road traveled and driving style) – impractical. A large machine may require several workers to make it function, making individual ownerships more difficult to delineate than in the taxicab case. In the absence of constraints on individual behavior, many –

---

[7]The mechanics of how a free attribute available to a transactor will be used under fixed pay and under a share contract were presented in Chapter 3.

perhaps all — of the attributes of such a machine will be owned in common, and incentives for such activities as careful handling and maintenance may then be greatly weakened. An office building may accommodate many workers. Here, common-property problems such as those regarding the use of corridors and access to utilities need taking care of; still, because different individuals can be assigned distinct parts of the structure, individuals' rights can be reasonably well delineated, and hence the users can belong to more than one organization.

The preceding examples include common-property problems that may arise when the ownership of goods is divided among individuals. They also illustrate that the severity of capture problems varies from one case to another, and that the physical character of assets may affect organization. Indeed, the severity of capture problems is not uniform for different attributes of a single piece of equipment. Because different attributes of a piece of equipment are not equally susceptible to capture, it may be advantageous to handle its different attributes differently. The ownership of a capital good, then, is not expected always to be vested in a single person or in a single organization; instead, the ownership of individual attributes of equipment is expected to be structured to minimize the capture loss. Ownership of a piece of equipment will sometimes be divided and may take different forms. Those attributes that are susceptible to serious common-property problems will tend to be owned by organizations set to control these problems, and attributes of the equipment that are relatively free from such problems will tend to be individually owned.

Because large pieces of equipment often have major attributes that are susceptible to common-property problems, they will, by the hypothesis here, be owned by some centralizing organization, an organization that may be called a firm. This firm may appear to be a reiteration of the conventional firm, enjoying a scale economy in the use of equipment. Indeed, the firm here, like the received, textbook firm, does enjoy economies of scale in its line of operations. However, the product produced by the firm here is, unlike the traditional firm's product, defined by the nature of the common-property problems it encounters. Equipment contributes to production of output; and when the separate ownership of different attributes of a single piece of equipment is economical, the output will not necessarily be produced by a single firm. The capital good "large office building" is a striking example of an asset whose attributes are owned by a number of owners.

Large office buildings are owned and used in a radically different way from that implied by the standard model. The owner of a large office building is the individual or the organization holding title to it. Nevertheless, that owner does not usually retain the rights to all attributes of the building. Her or his ownership is circumscribed. The individuals working in an office building are seldom the employees of the owner of the building, and the firm holding title to the building is seldom the firm that actually uses it. Indeed, sometimes the sole service a title holder supplies is the coordination of the contracts that govern the use of the building.

The structure of rights over a large office building is complex. The title holder usually rents out office space, thereby relinquishing to the tenants a subset of rights she or he has previously held; and the renters – the tenants – become owners of these rights. Other parties are often granted rights to other attributes of the building. If the building has been mortgaged, the mortgage-holding bank has, most likely, imposed restrictions on the building owner, thereby making itself the owner of a subset of rights, and it therefore becomes a residual loser in case the building owner is unable to make mortgage payments. If the landlord has retained a janitorial service, the service supplier assumes liability for her or his operation, and is, in turn, the owner of another subset of rights. Owners of still other rights may be enumerated; I shall discuss one more right – that associated with fire insurance – in greater detail than the rest, because the fire-insurer's role as residual claimant is easy to grasp (and because it seems counter to many economists' perception of what the function of fire insurance is).

The office-building owner, by paying an insurance premium, induces the insurer to assume the consequences of fire. In essence, a fire insurer *acquires ownership* over the attribute of fire incidence.[8] The insurer is a claimant of a particular residual because she or he will lose from the occurrence of fire and will gain from its non-occurrence. The insurer will gain by implementing effective fire-prevention measures, since as a residual claimant she or he takes the consequences of undertaking such steps. I shall discuss the fire-insurance arrangement further in a section on the structure of organizations.

Given that several organizations hold rights over an asset such as an office building, the question arises as to the principle that governs the allocation of these rights. I suggest that the structure of rights is designed to allocate ownership of individual attributes among parties in such a way that the parties who have a comparative advantage in managing those attributes that are susceptible to the common-property problem will obtain rights over them. For instance, it is expected that in a condominium in which all the units are located in one building, apartment owners will allocate the ownership of the effects of fire and of plumbing problems to the management, whereas where the individual units consist

---

[8] The expected value of such ownership is negative, and so the insurer makes a negative payment (receives a premium) in order to acquire the right.

of separate structures, the individual owners will tend to own (or to transact for) these attributes. Such a shifting of functions implies that the range of activities a firm undertakes is not constant. It is desirable, then, to reexamine, albeit briefly, the relationship between the industry's supply function and the firm's cost function.

Incorporating the notion of divided ownership of equipment in the analysis of the firm and the industry does not necessarily alter the resulting market supply curve, but it radically alters its construction. The received analysis might commence with the firms providing the service of the use of office space. The services of "use of office space" are actually obtained from a vertical array of firms. The precise nature of the product each of these firms supplies is not, in general, constant over time, and is not identical to what similar firms in the industry are providing. For instance, some landlords supply free parking, others charge for parking separately, and still others avoid getting directly involved with supplying this service to tenants by transferring the right to the service attributes to independent operators. Correspondingly, there is no reason to expect that as the market price of the use of office space rises, all existing firms contributing to the market supply will get larger: The structure of firms cannot be thought of as independent of market conditions. Organizations are structured to solve an array of common-property problems, the severity of which depends, in part, on the prices of inputs and outputs. At this point it is premature to analyze fully the vertical or the horizontal integration of such firms. One should address instead the question of how people contract in order to maximize the value of their resources.

The argument presented in this section points out that the severity of the common-property problem is not uniform over a piece of equipment and that the divided ownership of the equipment permits various common-property problems to be handled separately, both from one another and from less severe instances. Each problem can get its custom-made treatment; areas from which the common-property problem is absent may escape the treatment designed to cope with common-property issues. The analysis that isolates individual common-property problems is only the first step toward the analysis of the solution of such problems. The next task is to discuss steps that can be taken to reduce the costs associated with common-property problems.

MITIGATING COMMON-PROPERTY PROBLEMS

The simplest way to contain the common-property problem in the use of equipment is to modify the equipment. If equipment size is scaled down to fit a single operator, the capture problem disappears, the problem of raising capital is eased, and the need for organization is obviated. The sacrifice associated in economies of scale, however, is often too large.[9]

Another method of containing capture costs, one that involves organization, is the imposition of restrictions on the users of equipment in order to reduce their excessive and careless use of it. The wage contract constitutes a major application of this method. By virtue of its basic feature – reward for time – that contract abates the common-property problems of an attribute (or a set of attributes). Were the wage contract strictly an exchange of time for money, employees would simply provide time without ever lifting a finger as long as work effort did not generate utility directly. Such employees, therefore, would not harm the equipment around them. The wage contract is obviously more than an exchange of time for money; employers must induce employees to perform various tasks at some minimal pace. Given job specifications and the level of supervision, workers will satisfy the requirements at the least cost to themselves. They will necessarily put out less effort than self-employed workers do, because, on the margin, employees are not remunerated for effort. Since workers under a wage contract are not paid for output, their incentive to overuse whatever equipment they are provided with is curtailed.[10] Employers, however, must be able to get their workers to produce; for instance, employees may be required to keep pace with equipment.

Were workers' and machines' exertions proportional to each other, workers' maximization would suffice to avert overworking of the equipment. Some substitution between workers' and machines' exertion, however, seems possible; at the very least, workers' incentive to service their equipment is curtailed. Therefore, job specifications and supervision must take into account such opportunities and make provision for equipment maintenance. Because wage contracts (along with other contract provisions) remove workers' incentive to overuse equipment, many workers may all work with a single piece of equipment and not treat it as common property. Whereas the received treatment of labor provides no explanation of why time is the dominant unit by which labor is exchanged, the role of the wage contract in avoiding equipment abuse may explain, in part, its widespread use.

Workers who sell their labor services by way of a wage contract are engaged in a constrained transaction: They agree to obey a certain range of instructions. Their employers, in turn, also accept various constraints

---

[9]The potential for multiple shifts is also sacrificed as long as the equipment is used by only one person. This potential is sometimes also sacrificed within firms, presumably to enhance employees' accountability and so ease remaining common-property problems.

[10]The wage contract may also be used to control equipment abuse when a piece of equipment is operated by one person but owned by another.

on their own behavior, such as agreeing to a maximum equipment speed, providing coffee breaks, and allowing grievance procedures. The labor contract is but one of many contracts imposing constraints on the transactors; such constraints are an integral part of any organization. The employment contract and the associated constraints may appear to lead to the theory of the firm. However, constrained transactions are also common to what is usually called the market, and therefore the absence or presence of constraint does not generate a clear distinction between operations in the market and in firms.

THE FIRM VERSUS THE MARKET: A FALSE DICHOTOMY

Both the Coase (1937) approach and the traditional approach group interactions among people into two categories: those carried out in the market and those carried out within the firm. In neither case is the classification exhaustive, but in both cases each of the two types of interaction seems important alone and stands in sharp contrast to the other. In each of the cases, activities within firms, unlike activities in the market, require organization.

In the traditional approach, firms buy inputs in the market and transform them into output, which is then sold in the market; specialization in production, then, is carried out by (and within) firms, and specialization in exchange is carried out by markets. Actually, as already discussed, under the assumption that firms or entrepreneurs possess a perfect knowledge of market conditions, of all attributes of inputs and outputs, and of the production function, organization within a firm is innocuous. Any within-firm, cross-owners operation is, in essence, an exchange and can also be performed in the market. Precisely the same results that are obtained by firms can be achieved without recourse to such organizations. For instance, any worker may operate as an independent entity, being remunerated strictly by the value of output (from which her or his damage to equipment is netted), because if the true value of any component of a worker's contribution can be costlessly assessed, then it can also be directly remunerated. There is no compelling reason for workers to become employees, rewarded indirectly by the hour. It is true that there is no harm in employing workers by the hour, because, under the given conditions, their hourly contribution can also be evaluated costlessly. But this equivalence between workers' employee status and independent status is precisely what renders such organization innocuous.

Coase adopts a radically different approach in attempting to explain why some activities are in the market, guided by prices, and others are in the firm, guided by orders. He argues that transacting in the market is costly and that operating within firms is a means of reducing the costs. Coase, however, does not follow through fully on his own assertion that market transactions are costly. In order to incorporate such costs into my analysis, a precise meaning must first be given to the term "market transaction."

Two distinct definitions of the term "market transactions" are seemingly consistent with the common understanding of the term. One is that they are properly and fully priced transactions, free, therefore, of distortions; in other words, in such transactions individual buyers and sellers bear the full costs of their actions. Now, whereas Coase does not explicitly suggest that transacting in the market involves distortions, the asserted costliness of such transactions *must* imply that some marginal equalities of the zero transaction cost model are violated.[11] It does not seem useful, then, to view market transactions as distortion-free. The other, not well-recognized, definition is that they are transactions that, once concluded, leave no obligations remaining between transactors. For the analysis of allocation problems, this second definition that market transactions are those without lingering obligations, that is, are governed by caveat emptor, is the more attractive of the two. I suggest that, when this definition of "market transactions" is adopted, the distinction between firm and market transactions retains little practical importance, since caveat emptor transactions are costly and govern only a small fraction of the total volume of trade.

It is useful to relate the argument I am presenting here to Cheung's (1983) contribution to the analysis of the firm. Cheung points out that the organizations falling under the label "firm" are diverse; that the wage contract does not sufficiently characterize them; and most important, that there is no satisfactory operational definition of the firm. He suggests that economists should abandon the firm as a vehicle of their analysis and should instead focus on contracts. Cheung, however, retains the distinction between firm transactions and market transactions. He says the " 'firm' is . . . a way to organize activities under contractual arrangements that differ from those of ordinary product markets" (p. 3). Given costly transacting, however, Cheung's point with regard to the firm fully applies to *all* non–caveat emptor transactions.

Since caveat emptor transactions are costly, they are used only under narrowly circumscribed conditions. Would-be buyers of commodities whose sale is subject to caveat emptor will not part with their money before either inspecting the commodities sufficiently to convince them-

---

[11]The view that aside from occasional "externalities" markets are free of distortions is pervasive. I believe that this view is at the root of all sorts of confusion, especially when particular distortions are considered to be exceptions and therefore to call for exceptional measures, when they are in reality instances of the general case.

selves that they are not throwing their money away, or, alternatively, satisfying themselves of the sellers' reputation, which requires that the sellers have previously invested in it. Transactions accompanied by sellers' obligations are an alternative to caveat emptor transactions; such transactions, however, are accompanied by restrictions on the transactors. The within-firms transactions, then, are not unique in imposing restraints on the participants.

In most transactions, particularly in highly valued ones, the sellers' obligations continue after the sale is completed. For instance, sellers often guarantee sales; they are also usually liable for product malfunction. Indeed, these two types of obligations often apply simultaneously, highlighting the fact that different attributes of a transaction are subject to distinct problems and are differently constrained. These obligations are parts of contracts that specify what each of the parties agrees to cede to the others. Contracts may also restrain the parties in order to enhance the meeting of those contract obligations that are not discharged at transaction time. Caveat emptor transactions are, of course, free of constraints. More important, the presence of the constraints means that resources are not allocated by price alone.[12] Implementing and policing constraints require an organization, and different kinds of constraints require correspondingly different organizations. Cheung's suggestion that we study the contracts governing what are considered to be firm operations should be extended to include all restrained operations, whether they are in the firm or in the market.

The employment contract, wherein a worker agrees to be ordered by her or his employer, is the one singled out by Coase to characterize the firm. The employment contract, however, is just one of an array of methods of constraining transactions. In the discussion of the tenancy contract in the last chapter I showed why the share contract and the fixed-rent contract are no more in the market than is the wage contract, even though only the latter is said to identify a firm's operations. Many other contracts do not seem to fall neatly in one rather than in another category. When one uses the services of an automobile mechanic or sees a doctor or receives a house call from a plumber, the services rendered are usually considered to be in the market. Bills for such services are sometimes stated in units that approximate the desired output (the fees here could be for flushing a radiator, treating a sprain, or fixing a leak), seeming to place the transaction in the market. Other charges, however, are in terms of the providers' time, indicating that these are employment – seemingly firm – contracts. Classifying transactions into those in the market and those within the firm, then, is

[12]Because of the costs of conducting market exchange, market prices convey only partial information on the terms of exchange.

not very illuminating; transactions within the firm are too varied to be usefully placed in a single category. It is instructive, however, to explain the types of contracts expected to be employed in different situations and, in particular, the structure of contracts of large organizations. Before turning to this organizational problem, I shall relate the problem of variability to the Coase Theorem.

VARIABILITY, LIABILITY, AND THE COASE THEOREM

In his momentous article on social cost, Coase (1960) brings the question of liability to the fore and demonstrates what has come to be known as the Coase Theorem: that when property rights are well defined and transacting is costless, resources will be used where they are most valued, regardless of which of the transactors assumes liability for her or his effects on the other.[13] Coase does not address the question of the conditions under which liability problems arise. Now, it is essential to recognize that variability is a necessary condition for liability; liability poses a problem only in the presence of a variability that is too costly to eliminate. A producer of bottled soda would not bother with his product if he knew that all the bottles would explode. A slight but *uniform* defect is a liability; the problem such a liability creates, however, can be fully resolved ahead of time by adjusting the price of the product. In both cases, the product is not subject to variability and liability problems are absent, as are problems of delineating property rights.

If property rights are to be well defined, a person who benefits another must be fully rewarded by the beneficiary, and a person who harms another must pay full compensation to the harmed person. By this criterion, a contributor to variability must assume the full effect of her or his actions if rights are to be fully delineated. This condition is satisfied in two of the cases of cooperation between owners of land and of labor discussed in the last chapter. In one, land, but not labor, is uniform, and the contract between owners is of fixed rent; in the other, labor and labor effort, but not land, are uniform, and the contract is of fixed wage. In these two cases, transaction costs are not assumed to be zero, but property rights are well defined because the method of pay satisfies the condition that the factor owner who can affect the outcome bears the full effect of her or his actions.

In the two cases, rights are well defined *only* because the appropriate contracts are used; that is, the contracts are for *particular* assignments of liability. If, when land is uniform but labor is not, the fixed-wage contract

[13]Costless transacting, however, is a sufficient condition for clearly defining property rights, rendering redundant the requirement that property rights be well defined.

was the contract chosen, then neither would property rights be well defined, nor would resource use be efficient. The allocation of variability here *determines* whether or not rights are well defined. Therefore, it is meaningless to state that if rights are well defined, resource allocation is efficient regardless of who is liable (or who bears the effect of variability).

In general, both parties to a contract can contribute to the variability in outcome. Since the individual effects cannot be costlessly isolated, property rights, as a rule, are not well defined. As a party's effect on the value of the outcome increases, rights will be better defined if that party assumes a larger share of the variability of outcome. This is the hypothesized guiding principle behind the formation of those contracts that govern the operations of an organization and behind the determination of when a party will assume a larger share of the variability, thereby becoming more of a residual claimant.

THE INNER STRUCTURE OF ORGANIZATIONS

Organizations are the collections of contracts that govern the operations of multiple resource owners. Given organizations' hypothesized role of resolving common-property problems, each subset of resource owners that is affected by a common-property problem is expected to have its own subset of contracts. The set of coordinated contracts that makes up the whole organization resembles the Alchian and Demsetz (1972) "nexus of contracts." The role of residual claimants in such organizations requires an elaborate discussion.

Each of the multitude of contracts a firm has with the various parties it deals with constitutes a component in the allocation of the overall variability in income the firm faces. A party is expected to assume more of the variability, that is, become more of a residual claimant, as its effect on the mean outcome increases. Efficiency is the sole motivator for this hypothesis (since the model here assumes risk neutrality): The parties who assume more of the variability when their inclination to affect outcome increases simply guarantee a larger share of their own action, which could otherwise become damaging. When the parties guarantee their action, their incentive to take advantage of exchange partners is curtailed.

Consider the variability surrounding the operations of a firm engaged in production of a commodity. Ultimately someone must bear the effect of variability in the outcome of the firm's activity, just as someone must bear the outcome of any action. Any activity resulting in variable outcome, then, must have one or more residual claimants. Take as an example a firm that may wish to contract with a fire-prevention specialist to provide fire-prevention services. Under risk neutrality, which I assume, the sole objective of such a transaction is the minimization of the expected net loss from fire. A specialist who charges a fixed fee for her or his service provides fire insurance at a fixed premium. Such an insurer will lose from fires and is therefore motivated to take actions to reduce the level of fire losses, such as minimizing fire hazards, conducting fire drills, and supplying speedy fire fighting when fire occurs. Full insurance coverage implies that the insurer is the sole residual claimant of the fire hazard facing the firm.[14] If coverage is not full, then both the insured and the insurer are, to various degrees, fire-hazard residual claimants. It is unlikely that only the insurer can affect the incidence of fire and the loss from it; the behavior of the insured is also expected to affect fire losses. The insured usually decides on such questions as where and how flammable materials are kept; whether or not cigarette smoking is discouraged; and how well the employees of the insured keep fire escapes unobstructed. Both parties, then, contribute to the mean effect of fire hazard, and both are expected to bear some of the effect.

As applied to this case, my prediction is that when a party's contribution to the mean loss due to fire decreases, the fire-insurance contract will be modified to decrease that party's *share* of the fire losses. For instance, suppose that motors are used in the insured operations. A switch by the insured, due, say, to a change in relative fuel prices, from gasoline motors, which are a serious fire hazard, to electric motors, which are less of a fire hazard, constitutes a reduction in the insured's contribution to fire hazard. The insured's share in the income variability due to fire hazard ought to be reduced; in this case, the insured's coinsurance rate should be lowered.[15]

The presence of numerous input owners can affect the mean outcome of a firm's operations. Depending on their contracts, each of these owners will bear more or less of the effect of variability associated with their inputs. As just discussed, a firm that buys fire insurance, as many firms do, is making fixed payments in order to reduce the variability it faces. Purchasing any kind of insurance explicitly transfers effects of variability. Innumerable other methods are also available to subdivide the variability components in the outcome of firms' operations.

The contractual obligation employers assume to pay wages to employees is conventionally thought to insulate these owners of labor services from the effects of variability. The term "wage contract," however, does not connote a single arrangement; a menu of wage contracts from which

---

[14]For coverage to be full, it must include, besides direct losses, such effects as those due to lost business and to inconvenience.

[15]Insurers indirectly perform another service: the policing of employees' diligence in reducing expected fire losses. An increase in premiums (relative to other premiums) signals to owners that their employees have become too lax. For a related discussion, see Hall (1986).

to choose is available. Workers may be hired on a daily basis and be paid a spot wage; they may be hired for life for a fixed sum; or they may be hired on some intermediate basis. In addition, the employment contract may contain such features as escalation clauses, schemes for severance payment, and requirements for advance notice of layoffs. Each of these contracts exposes workers to a variability that differs from that to which they are exposed by any of the others. Employers are similarly subject to variability that depends on the particular contract chosen, because they are exposed to the complementary or remaining variability.[16]

The considerations that apply to labor similarly apply to both the prices and the quantities of all other purchases and to sales. Regarding variability in quantities, firms may, for instance, purchase their trucks and then bear the effects of varying durabilities across trucks; or they may rent the trucks, shifting the variability in longevity to rental agents. Similarly, employers who pay uniform hourly wages to non-uniform workers bear the variability in performance among the workers, whereas workers who are paid by the piece bear more of the variability. As a final example, buyers bear the effect of variability in product quality for purchases subject to caveat emptor; if caveat emptor does not apply, sellers bear at least some of that variability.

If the function of ownership is indeed to assume responsibility for variability in order to increase joint income, then holders of corporate equity are the residual claimants to only part of the variability in the operation of a firm; a whole array of other transactors assume the effects of components of the variability. Fire insurers are the residual claimants to the (insured) effects of fire; the commodity supplier who has signed a long-term fixed-price contract guarantees the constancy of the price of her or his commodity and is thus the residual claimant to fluctuations in that price; the buyer of bad debts is the bearer of the variability in the repayment rate. A salesperson rewarded by commission is more of an owner than one who is paid a fixed wage; an in-house lawyer is less an owner of the outcome of legal action than is an outside lawyer paid by the hour, who is, in turn, less an owner of the variability in outcome than is the lawyer operating on contingency. The greater the ability of a demander of legal services to affect the outcome by her or his own behavior, the greater is her or his expected share in outcome variability.

It does not seem possible to state precisely which activities should be designated activities of the firm and which should not. Only when transactions are subject to caveat emptor is the separation between transactors complete. Caveat emptor transactions, however, are the exception rather

---

[16]Each contract will induce a different performance. The total variability, then, also depends on the contract chosen.

than the rule. In all other transactions, the contracts between the parties impose restrictions on their behavior, leaving the transactions within the firm to some extent. The strength of such ties is not uniform, and thus some contracts are more in the firm than others. Here, too, it is most useful to try to determine conditions under which the ties will be strengthened or weakened.

THE ABILITY TO ASSUME VARIABILITY, AND THE ROLE OF EQUITY CAPITAL

In the discussion of the assignment of variability among transactors, I have concentrated on transactors' inclination to affect the outcome of their transactions. The levels of transactors' own wealth, however, constrain their guaranteeing ability and affect the nature of the obligations among them. The payment promised to a factor employed for a fixed rate of pay may diverge at any time interval from the spot market price of that factor. Therefore, the rate of payment to a party who is offered (relatively) fixed pay will part of the time fall short of the market value of the services supplied and will the remainder of the time exceed the value of these services. When the reward falls short of the party's contribution, that party must agree, and be able, to finance the difference; when the reward exceeds the contribution, the other party to the exchange must agree, and be able, to finance the difference. The dependability of parties in financing these differences depends on guarantees, and factor owners differ in their ability to guarantee their actions. I shall illustrate the nature of such problems for the contracting of labor services.

Suppliers of labor services are severely restricted in their insuring ability, particularly given the illegality of slavery. It might be advantageous for the workers to become the residual claimants where their actions are especially costly to supervise. The value of the associated variability, however, might be larger than workers are able to guarantee. Some liability problems and the operation of very valuable equipment, such as jet airplanes, seem to fall in this category. Owners of equity capital may then assume the guaranteeing role and require that workers be constrained so that their incentive to induce liability problems or to damage equipment is curtailed. Here, again, the wage contract and the accompanying supervision may be used. Owners of labor can readily finance one particular obligation – to supply labor services when the market wage exceeds the contract wage; this they can do by simply showing up at work.[17] Owners of labor, therefore, are more likely to enter into contracts in which they

---

[17] In other words, workers simply continue to work at the contract wage, and the difference between that wage and the market wage accrues to their employers.

are required to guarantee the difference between their market wage and their actual wage than they are to enter into contracts that require them to guarantee other possible effects of their behavior. Owners of productive factors other than labor may also lack sufficient wealth to guarantee their actions fully. Equity capital, however, is different from other productive factors in this regard.

Equity capital is a factor *specializing* in guarantees. The buyers or employers of any productive factor are able to affect the outcome of the transaction and are therefore expected to guarantee their actions. The better is their ability to provide such guarantees, the better are the contracts that can be reached. For instance, certain types of labor may be most productive if employees are provided with substantial on-the-job training. Workers may be reluctant to invest in themselves unless employers guarantee their future wages. Equity capital can provide such a guarantee, and, ceteris paribus, the higher is the outstanding equity capital, the more nearly optimal the level of training will be. Equity capital is productive, then, and its amount will be expanded to the point where the cost of expanding it by one more unit brings an equally valued improvement in contract terms of the employed factors, including borrowed capital. *The guaranteeing function, therefore, determines* (at least in part) *the optimal level of equity capital.* A firm may be viewed as the set, or nexus, of contracts guaranteed by the equity capital.

The share contract is a form of organization at the other end of the spectrum from the equity firm. The equity firm guarantees its contracts by equity capital. Under the sharing contract, the cooperating resource owners simply divide whatever the outcome of their efforts turns out to be. The problem of guaranteeing factor remuneration is then absent (as it is among stockholders). Sharing is likely to emerge when the provision of guarantees among factors is difficult (as is the case when the cooperating factors consist mostly of workers) and when their output is easy to divide.

SUMMARY

The received model, in which firms are essentially a production function phenomenon and the minimum point of the average cost function determines the competitive firm size, is unsatisfactory. If transaction costs were zero, such firms could arise but would be of trivial importance. Moreover, there seems to be virtually no correspondence between such firms and those actually observed. Following Coase (1937), I suggest that firms, or at least organizations, result from positive transaction costs.

Because of the complexity of transactions and the costliness of metering and policing their attributes, not all attributes are priced. Unpriced attributes tend to be excessively used and inadequately provided. Using unpriced attributes is equivalent to placing the attributes in the public domain. In order to reduce the associated losses, transactors will agree to constrain themselves; and effecting constraints requires organization.

Contractors must agree on a formula to allocate the outcomes of their interactions. When such outcomes are variable, the contractors allocate the variability among themselves. I argue that such allocation is at the heart of organization. The central principle underlying an organization is that the greater is the inclination of a transactor to affect the mean outcome, the greater is the claim on the residual the transactor will assume. Most activities are subject to many sources of outcome variability, and different resource owners or sets of owners may assume different parts of the variability. Guarantees are required in the presence of variability; the owners of equity capital who guarantee the contracts of various other resource owners within a single organization may be viewed as the owners of the corresponding firms. The improvement in contract terms more equity can induce is one of the many results of the transaction cost approach to organization, results that are not within the scope of the received theory of the firm.

5

The formation of rights

Now that the causes of allowing properties to be kept in the public domain have been analyzed, we are prepared to address the issue of the formation of rights. It is tempting to try to trace the pattern of property rights holding that exists today back to its origins to figure out how and why it came about. Such an effort, however, would be futile. The ability to consume commodities, including those necessary to sustain life, implies the possession of rights over them. One cannot expect, then, to discover any evidence of a pre–property rights state, and it is, in fact, not possible to endow a pre–property rights state of affairs with meaning. In order to gain a toehold on the evolution of property rights, one must start with a world where some rights are already in place, resorting to something less dramatic than, but similar to, the physicists' "Big Bang." Given that some rights already exist, it is possible to explore the evolution of such rights with respect to changes in economic conditions and legal constraints.

Inferences about the creation of property rights may be drawn through studying instances of anarchy or violent upheaval that required a radical act of rights redefinition. A spectacular example is that of the California gold rush, described and analyzed in fascinating detail by Umbeck (1977). Rich deposits of California gold were discovered in 1848, when California was under U.S. military occupation, just days before the signing of the peace treaty between the United States and Mexico. The gold-bearing land was not privately owned, and according to the treaty it became the property of the U.S. government. The United States finalized the transfer of power from Mexico to itself by abolishing the Mexican law pertaining to mining rights on government land, but failed to replace that law with any other until 1866. Thus, there was a complete absence of legal constraints governing the gold-bearing land in California. During this state of anarchy, thousands of fortune seekers, including many American military stationed in California who deserted their posts, descended on the Sierra foothills to prospect for gold. These gold seekers quite peacefully established rights over the deposits in one mine after another and adapted to new circumstances as they arose.

Umbeck's study, nevertheless, does not describe a primordial creation of rights. Instead it is concerned with the private creation of legal institutions where those previously provided by the state have ceased to be available. In another study, Umbeck (1981) is careful to note that, as chaotic as the gold rush was, some rights were defined all along in practice, particularly those to human assets and to personal belongings, which included guns.

Although the process of forming rights to the gold-bearing land was not subject to much violence, it consumed substantial amounts of resources. Rights delineation was exceptionally difficult to effect under gold-rush conditions because of the high costs of relevant information. The situation the gold seekers encountered was entirely novel. Little information was available to determine the precise criteria by which disputes would be settled and ownership ascertained. In the absence of state courts and of the known procedures under which courts operated, predicting who would win any particular dispute was rather difficult. Rights that are initially in the public domain become well defined when it is possible to determine who the ultimate owner will be. The conditions of the California gold rush made this determination exceptionally costly.

The very success of Umbeck's study derives, in part, from the uniqueness of the California gold-rush situation. Umbeck is able to explain the role of violence, or more accurately, of the threat of violence, when the state's authority is absent. His results, however, do not apply easily to more orderly circumstances. As a rule, in an already functioning society the creation of rights is an ongoing process. Rights are created in the presence of state authority, which has a comparative advantage over private individuals in the use of violence and which tends to discourage its private use. When a state authority is in place, the role of allocation devices other than violence is greatly enhanced. As I shall argue, property rights are *constantly* created and abandoned, and therefore there is a need for an analysis that fits continuing, smooth changes in conditions.

THE COMMON-PROPERTY/PRIVATE PROPERTY DICHOTOMY

With a few exceptions, economists until recently had not explicitly adopted a property rights framework from which to analyze economic problems. The earliest and most notable exception is Frank Knight's discussion of social cost (1924). In his analysis of the use of roads he clearly demonstrated the role of ownership. Several decades later, Scott

Gordon (1954) analyzed in a similar vein the common-property problem of fishing in international waters. After Knight, and even subsequent to Gordon's contribution, economists still did not do much with property rights. Economists' infrequent use of property rights considerations may reflect a belief that such considerations are unlikely to produce useful results. Indeed, because most property does not appear to be common property and, more important, because the transformation of what is clearly considered common property to what is clearly considered private property is rarely observed, property rights notions, as expounded, do not seem to be especially useful. The perception that property rights considerations are not useful in the analysis of resource allocation seems to stem from an all-or-none view of rights. Both Knight and Gordon assumed in their analyses that property rights are either present and perfectly well defined or that they are totally absent. They neglected the possibility of an intermediate state in which rights are only imperfectly defined.

The usual characterization of commodities as homogeneous entities, often with just one attribute, makes it easy to conclude that commodities are either owned or not owned and that there are no intermediate states of ownership. Such a view seems to have been bolstered by equating economic rights with legal rights and by treating the latter as being either present or absent. Moreover, the position usually taken has been that property rights are largely, perhaps entirely, created and enforced by government. Correspondingly, cases in which rights are left in the public domain have traditionally been viewed as the government's fault.[1] Knight and Gordon implied that if the government had turned roads or fisheries into private property, the associated common-property dissipation would have disappeared. This view is easy to accept if one accepts that commodities are one-dimensional, either owned or not owned. The existence of theft has been recognized as an exception to the view that rights are perfectly well defined. The notion that rights are not well defined *in general* has not, however, been pursued.

IMPERFECTLY DELINEATED RIGHTS

The delineation of property rights is subject to individuals' optimization; delineation consumes resources, and perfect delineation is prohibitively costly. Property rights, then, are never perfectly defined. Moreover, transacted commodities have many attributes, and the rights to different attributes of a given (physical) commodity or to different attributes of a

---

[1]Similarly it is often asserted that it is the government's duty to protect its citizens against theft.

transaction are not all equally well defined. The government, as a rule, participates in defining and in protecting private rights. Individuals, however, have a comparative advantage over the government in many of these activities and actually undertake most of them. Correspondingly, individuals' behavior must be considered in the study of rights formation.

The seed for the analysis of rights creation in an ongoing society was planted in Demsetz's (1967) study of the Montagnais Indians of Labrador. Demsetz's point is so simple that it appears to be self-evident: He showed that new rights are created in response to new economic forces. One implication of such a view is that rights in the sense of the ability to gain from property are largely a matter of economic value rather than of legal definition. Demsetz hypothesized that as the value of a common-property resource increases, people are more likely to establish rights over it. Specifically, he noted that prior to the Europeans' arrival in Labrador, when the value of beaver pelts was low, beaver habitats were held as common property. When the European market became accessible, the value of beaver pelts increased and beaver habitats were converted to private property. Demsetz did not, however, explore the nature of the break between the old and the new concept of rights, and, despite the novelty of his observations, he has failed to follow them through systematically.[2] Though some economists (and other social scientists) have applied Demsetz's ideas, they have not extended his methodology. I have chosen to expand and elaborate on this embryonic analysis of the formation of rights in order to show how individuals routinely delineate rights more or less carefully as the value of these rights increases or declines.

People acquire, maintain, and relinquish rights as a matter of choice. Individuals take such actions directly in the private sector and indirectly, through the state, in the public sector.[3] People choose to exercise rights when they believe the gains from such actions will exceed their costs. Conversely, people fail to exercise rights when the gains from owning properties are deemed insufficient, thus placing (or leaving) such properties in the public domain. What is found in the public domain, therefore, is what people have *chosen* not to claim. As conditions change, however, something that has been considered not worthwhile to own may be newly perceived as worthwhile; conversely, what was at first owned may be placed in the public domain.

Assuming ownership is not attenuated, the legal owners of commodities are free to exercise their rights over their commodities in any (legal) way they wish. What causes an imperfect delineation of rights, then, is

---

[2]In the same article, Demsetz seems to vacillate between the positivist view that rights are created in response to economic conditions and the normative view that government should enhance private rights.

[3]Rights exercised through the public sector include those vis-à-vis other countries.

owners' choice not to exercise all of their rights. Since rights that are not exercised are placed in the public domain, it follows that people deliberately place some of their properties in the public domain. For instance, both restaurant owners who supply their patrons with "free" salt and owners of movie theaters who charge the same price for better and for worse seats, thereby providing the differential free of charge, place some valued properties in the public domain. Patrons capture the rights to free salt by consuming it and consume it to the point where its marginal value to them is zero. Moviegoers capture the right to the better seats by getting to the theater early enough to preempt the occupation of such seats by others, with the value of waiting time of the marginal person in the queue equal to the difference in the value of seats. In both cases, owners set prices at high enough levels to cover their costs; however, they still relinquish the marginal units to the public domain, since in neither case does the marginal charge paid by the patron equal the cost of the marginal unit.[4]

Owners are not prohibited by law from imposing marginal charges for each of their commodities' attributes; rather, for some attributes, they deem the returns to be less than the costs. The costs of imposing marginal charges consist of measuring or metering and policing. Were such charges imposed, the returns for the restaurant owners would take the form of higher prices (net of the cost of the salt) received for meals they provide; the theater owners would be rewarded by higher revenues from theater tickets. Buyers, of course, would have to pay these higher prices, but their net valuation would be still higher. The owners, however, deem some of their rights too expensive to exercise and choose to place them in the public domain.[5]

These two examples illustrate cases where attributes are placed in the public domain by their owners. The phenomenon is ubiquitous.[6] Salt is just one of the many "free" attributes available to restaurant patrons. Another is patrons' opportunity to eat at rush hour while seldom paying to the owner a differential above the non–rush-hour price (and while capturing the valued rush-hour time, as a rule, by waiting or by rushing ahead of others). Patrons also do not pay, on the margin, for the amount of time they spend in the restaurant and for the level of commotion they

[4]Since owners cannot capture such values without incurring even greater costs, their actions are not dissipating.

[5]A similar discussion is presented in Alchian and Allen (1977); see esp. chap. 5. Conversely, the prescription that all rights should be made private is inconsistent with individual maximization and is, at best, innocuous.

[6]Chapter 3 includes a discussion of attributes that are placed in the public domain for each of the tenancy contracts.

create. Many similar opportunities are available to supermarket shoppers, who can also capture the value of better-than-average produce or meat by increasing their efforts at selection. Finally, when renters of equipment are charged by the day, the intensity of use, itself multidimensional, is a free attribute.

The claim that rights will be better delineated when the returns from more accurate pricing increase is not correct, although it seems obvious enough at first. It is true that when the price people are willing to pay for the service placed in the public domain increases, returns from its better delineation also increase. If, for instance, the value of all theater tickets were to be doubled, the difference in valuation between a bad and a good seat would double, too, and therefore the return from pricing the difference would increase. As pointed out by Umbeck (1981), however, the costs of policing would also increase, since in the new situation the gain from theft would be higher: People would gain more from stealing the difference, by buying tickets for the low-priced seats, for instance, and then attempting to occupy the higher-priced ones. There is no a priori reason to suggest that policing expenditures should increase more slowly than will the gains from more detailed pricing.

Whereas the incorporation of theft into the analysis negates the last paragraph's qualitative conclusion regarding the conditions for better delineation, the conclusion nevertheless seems to hold in practice because of choices available to owners. Owners can choose from a large menu of pricing structures in order to achieve a greater conformity to marginal cost pricing, and each of these ways incurs its own costs of theft. The costs of the extra policing required by some pricing methods may exceed the gains, but such is not necessarily the case for all methods, and owners control which methods to employ.[7] More important, the implication remains unambiguous for the cost side of the proposition. The incentive to steal is a function of the value of the target commodity but not of the costs of pricing or policing; when metering or policing costs decline, there is no reason to expect the gain from theft to increase. Thus, if the costs of metering and policing a service were to decline, rights to it would clearly be expected to become better delineated.[8]

---

[7]Cheung (1977) provides an example of an unusual policing method. He argues that theater owners in Hong Kong underprice the more expensive movie theater seats in order to get them fully occupied and that such occupancy constitutes a relatively cheap method of policing.

[8]A confirmation of this implication – that is, observing a more detailed price structure when the costs of policing fall – would also confirm that transactions consist of many attributes whose levels vary from one specimen to another; otherwise, one price per transaction would suffice.

Economic analysis of property rights

Owners of commodities may choose to retain them or to exchange them. Exchange is subject to contracts to which the parties, obviously, agree. It may be puzzling, then, that disputes over ownership erupt at all. In order to see what may cause disputes and how they are settled, we need preliminary discussion of the effects of changes in conditions where delineation is incomplete.

Commodity owners decide whether or not to place attributes in the public domain. Theater owners, for instance, may price all seats equally one week and adopt a more detailed pricing scheme the next; they are free to alter which rights they retain and which they relinquish, because they continue to own the asset. The sale of theater tickets constitutes a rental contract of space in theaters, and owners can form new contracts as older ones expire. When owning an attribute becomes preferable to placing it in the public domain, the commodity owner will make the appropriate contract changes at contract renewal time. However, if during the period while the old contract is still in force an attribute is already in the public domain, it can be claimed only by spending resources.

In the case of theater tickets, the status of those seats that increase in value while the old price is still in force is clear. The advertising of particular pricing schemes for specific durations is part of the contract between an owner and patrons. Any breach of contract aside, the rights to tickets at the old prices are relinquished by the owners for the advertised duration. These rights are not relinquished, however, to particular individuals. Since the value of the seats is higher than before, competition among patrons for these seats will intensify. When the value of the seats is higher, the gain from avoiding such resource-consuming competition is also higher, but as these rights are already in the public domain, it is not necessarily possible to avoid competing for them.

In the polar cases of a fully owned commodity (or of fully owned attributes) and of a commodity placed in the public domain, the commodities continue to be owned and unowned respectively when their values change. Disputes may occur in intermediate cases, that is, when contracts between pairs of parties simply fail to spell out stipulations to attributes that seemed to be of little value at contract time but whose value increases before the contract expires. Consider a landowner who rents out a piece of land with some trees on it. Suppose that at contract time the trees, which are not sufficiently valued to be explicitly mentioned in the contract, are simply ignored. Suppose further that while the contract is in effect, a highly valuable use for the lumber is discovered. Because rights to the lumber are not well defined, a conflict regarding its ownership may erupt.

The formation of rights

Regarding capture of the rights placed in the public domain, I asserted that whatever the criteria for capture are, individuals will meet them as long as the gains from doing so exceed the costs. These criteria are set to fit the particulars of the situation. In the case of the single-price movie theater, the criterion is time;[9] in that of the fixed-rent tenant whose contract does not constrain the extraction level of soil nutrients, the criterion is the appropriate method and intensity of cultivation. These criteria, however, do not necessarily remain intact when the gains from capture increase. In particular, parties who initially only implicitly relinquish rights to an attribute to the public domain may claim that they retain partial or complete rights to the attribute and may attempt to compete with their transacting partners in recapturing the relinquished rights.

In the case of a contract that does not clearly delineate some rights whose value has increased, a conflict may emerge. In these contracts the owners of assets relinquish to their exchange partners subsets of their rights to the assets. The initial owners, whose actions (or, more likely, inaction) have implied that they have relinquished rights to an attribute, may now contend that these rights are their own, but their transacting partners may make the same claim. These considerations apply most clearly when the parties operate explicitly under contract; they may also apply to informal contracts and to relationships such as those between neighbors. Consider neighbors who possess a hedge that separates their properties. Initially they may have elected, at least in practice, to leave the hedge in the public domain. Changes may induce them to attempt to capture some attribute of the hedge, however. For example, a rare bird may decide to build a nest there. Here, too, a dispute may emerge as the value of property previously placed in the public domain increases.

The transactors considered here are operating under a contract, or at least under an implicit one. One issue for them to consider is how the court might allocate the disputed rights and what costs the parties would incur in the attempt to influence these decisions. The parties will compare their predictions of court decisions and of the associated legal costs with those of such other methods of settling their disputes as arbitration or entirely private settlement and will select in each case the method they perceive as entailing the lowest cost.[10] Obviously, the parties' decision

[9]Theater owners have the choice between leaving seats within a single price class unmarked or marking them individually. In the former case, patrons must wait for the theater doors to open; in the latter case, they must wait for ticket sales to commence. Owners, then, decide on the mode of waiting.

[10]The would-be plaintiff in a court case has the power to force the court's resolution of a dispute. When a dispute is actually settled out of court, it is because a would-be plaintiff has perceived this alternative to be of lower cost than settling in court. The other disputant, however, may provide compensation, perhaps in the form of concessions, so that the method of settlement involving the lowest *total* cost will be selected.

affects rights delineation in their own case; indirectly, it affects delineation in general.

THE ROLE OF THE COURTS
IN THE DELINEATION OF RIGHTS

The courts participate in rights delineation in two ways. One is indirect: When the parties choose to settle their disputes without resorting to the courts, their action is influenced by their perception of how the courts would have acted in their dispute. The other way is direct: the actual settling of disputes by the courts. The rest of this section considers the second method of rights delineation.

In countries operating under common law, court rulings serve as precedents for new rulings. When private disputes end in common-law courts, resolution of the particular disputes ensues. Hence, these disputes produce a public good – the delineation of rights in situations similar to the one litigated: Since court rulings become precedents for similar cases, litigants are resolving others' disputes.[11]

Private contractors play several indirect but crucial roles that complement those of the court. One role relates to the gains that result from anticipating and avoiding disputes. Because disputes and litigation are costly, contractors gain if their contracts anticipate potential trouble spots and provide for them. When such contracts do nevertheless reach the courts, court rulings are likely to delineate rights clearly because they are dealing with carefully crafted contracts. This effect is enhanced by forces of selectivity, which determine, in part, which disputes will be litigated. Disputants go to court only if they are optimistic about the outcome (indeed, between them they must err in the direction of excessive optimism). A court ruling that is expected to be too ambiguous to truly settle a dispute deters the parties from litigating. Only if disputants expect a ruling to delineate rights clearly and thus incur few added future delineation costs will they litigate. Among all potential litigants in a given class of disputes, self-selection will bring out the actual litigants who expect a ruling that will clearly delineate rights that had previously been in dispute.

Private contracts affect the delineation of rights in one more way. As conditions change, contract stipulations that had been attractive in the past may cease to be useful. Since the common law tends to absorb features that recur in private contracts, it is likely to have incorporated into itself the features deemed attractive in the past. The courts are likely to rule accordingly in litigation where the parties have failed to stipulate

---

[11]Private rights are constrained by both common and by statutory law. I shall not discuss the forces that affect statutory law; that would require an analysis of legislative behavior, a task beyond the scope here.

70

on various features of their transactions and have therefore implicitly accepted the common-law stipulations. When writing new contracts, however, contractors may explicitly stipulate whatever they wish, and as long as the stipulations are not in conflict with basic principles of the law, the courts will respect the new stipulations. As new stipulations are written into contracts, the common law gets exposed to them, tends to take them into account, and gradually replaces the old, less desired stipulations with the preferred newer ones.

COMMON PROPERTY

I claimed that economists have tended to classify ownership status into the categories all and none, the latter being termed "common property" – property that has no restrictions placed on its use. The term originates from English villagers' practice of using certain areas for, among other things, collectively grazing their animals and cutting firewood. The current meaning of the term "common property" certainly does not fit the English villagers' actual practice, as shown by Dahlman (1980). Dahlman's description makes it clear that the village common was open only to the villagers, not to outsiders, and that the villagers' own rights were stinted: They did not have the right to add livestock to the herd at will or to cut whatever amount of wood they wanted. All were allowed to place in the herd only a set number of animals and all were restricted in the amount of wood they could cut. Whereas that land was held in common, its use was directly controlled by the villagers, partly through voting. It was certainly managed as private property.[12]

Regarding current practices, properties under government control are sometimes tagged as "common," or as being in the "public domain." It is improper, however, to view such properties as being unowned. Properties that in economic (rather than legal) terms are owned by no one are deprived of any value. The view is sometimes expressed that such properties would be positively valued were they diverted to private ownership. A closely related view is that the transfer of government property to private ownership will necessarily increase its value. A priori reasoning, however, is incapable of demonstrating that private ownership is necessarily more efficient than government ownership. If, as argued above, metering and policing are expensive, then private ownership, as compared with a zero transaction costs state, is never free of dissipation. So long as the use of public property is subject to restrictions,[13] as it usually is, one

[12]Dahlman supplies considerably more detail on the management of the common.
[13]Individuals' costs of using public property (e.g., for transportation equipment) are one instance of such a restriction that sometimes suffices to prevent complete dissipation.

cannot conclude that rights would be better delineated under private than they are under public ownership. The distinction between common property and property under government control will now be illustrated for the case of the private use of public roads.

Roads are economic goods typically held in the public sector. The conditions that implicitly underlie Knight's (1924) analysis of private ownership of roads are those such that private entrepreneurs can determine and collect the optimal prices and police the use of the roads costlessly. In practice, these costs must be considerable. In comparing private and public ownership of roads it must also be recognized that public roads are not in fact managed as common property. Besides restrictions on features such as the safety and size of vehicles, road users are required to pay various fees and taxes, the gasoline tax being the most significant.

The gasoline tax is a device for rationing road use; the higher the tax, the lower the demand for roads and the lower the level of congestion. As a rationing device it is rather blunt; it fails to distinguish, for instance, between peak-hour use and off-peak use, and it makes the wrong distinction, in terms of congestion costs users impose, between more- and less-fuel efficient cars. Because of the costliness of pricing, market prices are subject to similar shortcomings. Correspondingly, as mentioned earlier, in their pricing schemes restaurant owners fail to distinguish between peak and off-peak hours and between fast and slow eaters. It is incorrect to conclude on a priori grounds, then, that the value of roads will increase if they are made private.

The observation that an asset is in the public sector does not imply that it is routinely placed in the public domain. Such assets are owned; that is, their value is not entirely dissipated by people who attempt to capture that value. The a priori conclusion that making such assets private will get better use out of them is not warranted. An alternative proposition is that as the costs of, or the gains from, monitoring public sector attributes increase, their use is expected to be restricted more. Testing this proposition will at the same time test the more fundamental hypothesis that the maximizing forces in government are the same as in the private sector. The delineation of property rights to the North Sea among the surrounding countries will illustrate the discussion in the preceding few sections.

THE CONVERSION OF THE NORTH SEA
INTO OWNED PROPERTY

In 1958 the Convention on the Continental Shelf was signed in Geneva (Dam, 1965). The provisions of the convention divided among the countries bordering the North Sea[14] some of the commonly held attributes of that sea, particularly those related to minerals. Two factors were working to enhance the value of the North Sea in the years preceding the agreement. First, underwater drilling, which was becoming more widespread, was declining in cost; second, various signs were emerging that the region bore gas and oil.[15] The countries surrounding the North Sea could conceivably have unilaterally extended their territorial rights toward the middle of the sea. Oil companies, however, were not going to invest resources searching for oil unless they expected their ownership of what they might find to be secure. Discussion in the preceding sections suggests that as the value of the oil resources of the North Sea increased, rights over it were expected to be better delineated.

By reaching an agreement, the countries involved gained ownership of segments of the sea; they could exploit their sea rights directly or could grant them to private parties and let those private concerns exploit them. Subsequent events proved that the formal agreement and the accurate delineation of borders was ultimately of great value. When the North Sea countries convened to establish rights over the sea, no one knew yet where oil would be found, so it was easy to arrive at a formula that would give each country the territory near it without generating much dispute regarding the precise setting of borders. The formula actually selected was that any point on the sea (and on the sea bottom) belonged to the country to which the point was closest.

As it turned out, many of the major oil and gas discoveries lay close to the border between the Norwegian and the United Kingdom sectors. Since the border was precisely marked, ownership of these finds was not in dispute. There is little doubt, however, that without the agreement oil companies would not have searched in that area.[16]

MEANS OF ENHANCING RIGHTS

One reason attributes are placed in the public domain is that it is too costly to measure and police all the attributes of a transaction. Transactors may attempt to capture attributes that are not adequately measured, or they

[14] Belgium, Denmark, France, the Netherlands, Norway, the United Kingdom, and West Germany.

[15] For instance, gas was discovered in the Netherlands and beneath the waters near the United Kingdom.

[16] There is a deep trench in the Norwegian sector of the North Sea. Crossing the trench by pipeline is prohibitively costly. Some of the Norwegian oil deposits are on the United Kingdom side of the trench, making the United Kingdom seem to be a more natural owner of that area than is Norway. As is consistent with Coase, however, once rights were delineated there was little problem in developing the area. Indeed, some of the Norwegian oil is shipped by pipeline to the United Kingdom.

may engage in excess measurement in order to reduce capture costs. In order to maximize the gain from exchange, transactors are expected to seek ways to curb such costs. One such method is to exploit scale economies in measuring; another is to discourage duplicating measurements.

Some measuring and policing costs increase less than proportionately to the number of units in a transaction. For instance, as a rule, less unit measurement is necessary when all transacted units are obtained from a single manufacturing batch or from a given field than when they are obtained from several batches or from different fields. Similarly, when a capital asset is rented, the unit cost of measuring the rental services declines as the rental period gets longer. Determining how productive the asset is requires only one measurement, and determining how intensely it has been utilized requires just a pair of measurements – one at the beginning and one at the end of the rental period. The availability of such scale economies, with regard to both a transaction size and its duration, reduces the costs of rights delineation and, therefore, the loss otherwise associated with placing attributes in the public domain.

An entirely different method of lowering the costs associated with placing attributes in the public domain is to induce the parties to act as if the attributes were owned even if they are not. When supermarket shoppers are allowed to choose items such as apples, they are in a position to capture the value of the better apples, which are sold at the same price as the worse apples. Sellers take deliberate action to make the displayed apples appear uniform. Indeed, were all buyers to choose randomly from the available selection (and given competition among sellers), then the cost to consumers of apples of a given average quality net the expense of choosing would be less than it is when consumers actually do pick and choose.[17]

SUMMARY

By their own actions individuals are able to control and to affect the delineation of their rights over "their" property. Individuals will exercise such control as part of their maximizing process. Whenever individuals find the existing level of delineation to be unsatisfactory, they will alter it until they are satisfied. In the same sense that individuals are always in equilibrium with regard to their asset holdings, they are in equilibrium with regard to their rights over their assets. At any time, then, their rights are precisely so well defined that they do not wish to change them.

Economic conditions, however, are constantly changing, and with them the equilibrium property rights delineation is changing as well. As

[17]Barzel (1982).

rights to commodities possessed by individuals become more valuable, the individuals will delineate these rights more thoroughly. As the value of rights to commodities that lie in the public domain increases, people will spend more resources to capture them and to turn them into private property. Such transfer from the public domain to private ownership is sometimes effected by individuals and sometimes by the state.

When the value of rights to those commodities that are in the process of being exchanged increases, disputes between the exchange parties may emerge. The resolution of disputes results in delineation of the contested rights. The courts participate in the delineation of disputed rights, and the common-law courts interact with individuals in such determinations. Individuals choose whether or not to go to a common-law court, and they will litigate new cases until rights become, in their perception, well defined.

When the costs of metering and of policing assets or assets' attributes exceed the valuations, such assets or attributes will be relinquished into the public domain and become common property. Such common property, then, is property that people *choose* not to own. Both the English common and government property in general are valued, and their use is restricted; as a rule, they are not really common property.

6

Slavery

By the beginning of this century slavery had largely disappeared. But comparing slaves and free laborers and exploring the forces that permitted slavery to flourish in some circumstances and not in others not only provide insight into an extinct institution; such study also sheds light on contemporary ones, enhancing especially the understanding of policing and ownership practices.

THE SLAVE CONTRACT

Labor services, routinely exchanged in the market,[1] are subject to contract. The typical contract for the services of a free worker transfers a rather narrow, and usually short-term, set of attributes from the labor owner to its buyer. Slavery, too, may be viewed as a labor contract – one, however, that gave slave owners extensive rights over their slaves. In the case of forced slavery, the contract extended over the slave's entire time horizon. The voluntary slave contract typically specified a shorter duration and gave the owner fewer rights over the slave than did the forced slave contract.

Forced slavery was initiated by theft – free people were captured and, as the term suggests, were forced into slavery. Voluntary slavery was the result of an explicit contract – a contract to which both parties agreed, presumably with the belief that signing the contract would be beneficial to each. In some cases, voluntary slavery resulted from a loan default, when, for whatever reason, persons who posted themselves as collateral against debt defaulted and lenders took over the collateral, assuming ownership of the persons. Indentured servitude, a form of voluntary

---

This chapter is largely derived from Barzel (1977).

[1] The term "market" is used here, and throughout the remainder of the book, in its conventional meaning.

76

slavery, was a direct method of repaying loans. Such loans often served to finance the passage of the servant from Europe to America. To repay the loan, indentured servants worked in America for a number of years virtually as slaves. The duration of the servitude was determined in an auction in which the winning bidder was the person who bid the smallest number of years of service and bought the loan contract from its previous holder – often the captain of the passage ship; the servant worked out her or his debt for the final lender, usually an American farmer.

The term "contract" normally implies a voluntary relationship; indeed, a relationship from which both parties expect to gain. The term fits voluntary slavery well but forced slavery less well. Free persons, having been forced into slavery, obviously did not expect any gain from their change in status. Thus, if the term can apply at all to forced slavery, it applies only to the period of time after the persons have already become slaves. Even then, such usage stretches the definition of "contract" to its limit. Nevertheless, it will be seen that the notion of a slave contract is still useful in analyzing the institution of slavery.

SLAVES' SUPPLY OF LABOR

Obviously, slaves were extremely poor people. A recognition of their poverty is essential if various practices under slavery are to be understood. The intensity of slave labor may be explored through the conventional labor–leisure choice analysis. In Figure 6.1, a typical diagram for such an analysis, a free worker with budget MM will choose to be at point A, which lies on U, the highest indifference curve that the worker can attain. A person subject to a budget constraint MM obtains her or his entire income from the use of her of his own time. A budget constraint $M'M'$ implies that the individual has an income equal to the vertical distance between MM and $M'M'$ from sources other than the use of her or his own time. Similarly $M''M''$ indicates a negative non-labor income, that is, a debt-payment obligation. A positive income elasticity for leisure – a highly plausible relationship for a person whose earning power is low and who is a net debtor – implies an increasing supply of labor as the budget constraint shifts inward. Given such income elasticity, as the fraction of a person's potential labor income that must be used for debt repayment increases, the person increases her or his labor supply accordingly.[2]

---

[2]The supply of labor is constrained by the length of the day; it is also constrained by fatigue. The effect of fatigue is abstracted from Figure 6.1; in the presence of fatigue the budget line would not be a straight line. Also abstracted is the intensity of work that is usually taken as given but is actually a choice variable. Both issues are elaborated on in my 1974 article.

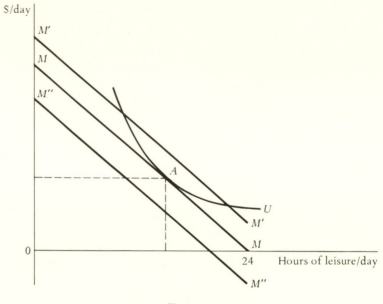

Figure 6.1

Workers incur maintenance expenditures – the minimal expenditures on items (e.g., food, medical care, shelter) that will sustain them at a given exertion level. Such expenditures most likely increase with the amount of labor supplied. Maximum income from work is the largest present value of labor income a worker is able to produce net of the present value of her or his maintenance expenditures. That particular labor effort associated with producing the maximum net present value also permits the largest possible debt payments. Such a level of exertion, then, defines the largest debt that a person can pay and still earn just enough to sustain herself or himself. A free person with a commensurate debt presumably will *choose* to operate at such a level of exertion. Policing costs aside, a forced slave can be viewed as a person who operates at exactly that point. The owner of a forced slave will require the effort that, net of maintenance expenses, will yield the highest present-value income stream. Thus, a forced slave may be compared to a free person who has contracted to operate in exactly the same way the slave is required to. Given that the slave (or her or his ancestors) was stolen, she or he operates under a contract the terms of which have just been described. Manumission is the act of buying out that contract.

In the era when the law permitted slavery, the question of manumission was pertinent. As indicated in the opening paragraph of this book, the

78

observation of self-purchase poses a major puzzle: How could a slave, another person's piece of property, purchase her or his own contract? In order to resolve this puzzle, transaction costs, in particular policing costs, must be considered.

THE COSTS OF SUPERVISION

Since slaves were the full-fledged property of their owners, all the income they could generate was legally their owners'. Owners who took anything from their slaves were simply taking something that was legally theirs to start with. Owners had the legal right to take; they also had the might. How could slaves, then, accumulate wealth, sometimes to an extent that enabled them to purchase their own contracts? Had both slaves' capabilities and the net output they produced been costlessly measurable, wealth-maximizing slave owners would indeed have extracted every last ounce of productiveness from their slaves. Under these conditions, conditions that would have permitted owners to be owners in the most complete sense of the word, it is ironic that the slave status itself would have been inconsequential. Had policing been costless, the owner could have let the debtor operate as a free person and still obtain the same income, for instance, by receiving an explicit debt payment of the same value as that generated by the slave's services without requiring a slave contract. The free person, however, would still have had to work exactly like a slave in order to be able to pay her or his debt.[3] Since in reality the evaluation of inputs and outputs is costly, policing is required to induce effort; as we shall see, accumulation by slaves is then possible.

When the net output of a free worker can be determined at low cost, it is advantageous for her or him to operate as an independent worker, since then no problems of incentive arise in motivating her or him to work. Such was not the case with slaves; the labor services slaves could provide belonged to their owners. Even when output was easily measured, slaves would have gained from producing less and thus had to be induced to produce more. The distinction between slaves' and free workers' incentive became even more acute for tasks that free workers performed by the hour. Free workers will do best if they can convince their future employers that they are more productive than they actually are, since, as it is difficult to ascertain their true productiveness, their wages will then be higher. Slaves, on the other hand, would have done best if they could have convinced their owners that they were no good, since little would then have been expected

[3]Under costless transacting not only would the slave status become devoid of significance, but forced slavery would never have arisen in the first place, since one person would never have captured the rights of others.

of them.[4] Slave owners, then, had to spend resources to figure out how productive the slaves were and how hard they could be driven and to actually supervise their efforts or output.

Assuming that the supervision of effort is subject to diminishing marginal productivity, owners would, in their supervision effort, have stopped short of extracting the maximum output of which slaves were capable.[5] The difference between slaves' maximum output and their actual output became, in practice, the slaves' property. It did not, as a rule, come in the same form as the product they produced for their owners, but mostly in reduced effort. Still, slaves were able to convert some of this potential into property, property that owners had an interest in protecting.

Owners had the choice between supervising their slaves' output, which is comparable to what employers have to do when the free workers they employ work by the piece, and supervising their effort, which is comparable to what employers have to do when they employ free workers by the hour. The latter required continuous supervision, since whenever slaves were not watched over they had little incentive to perform. The former required overseeing output as to its quantity, its quality, and, indirectly, its effect on other productive services such as equipment. Slaves' output supervision also required output quotas, since, left to their own devices, they would have produced as little as they could. Moreover, quotas could not have been set by simply observing past performance, since slaves' incentive to produce little during the demonstration period would have been strong indeed. Since quotas were subject to error, and since too high a quota would have resulted in the destruction of slaves, the quotas owners would have selected to maximize their own wealth were expected to leave their slaves with the difference between the quota and the maximum they could produce, a difference they could take advantage of. Since owners' confiscation of slaves' accumulation would have been equivalent to raising the quota, confiscation would have defeated the purpose for which the quota was set to begin with. In pursuit of their self-interest, owners permitted slaves to own and to accumulate.

Slaves seldom became rich. Nevertheless, the free time they were able to gain enabled them, among other things, to grow vegetables, to fish and hunt, and also to steal. Their owners and neighbors were ready buyers for what slaves had to sell. Slaves who were ultimately able to buy their contracts were, as a rule, household slaves, sometimes well-trained ones.

---

[4]Slaves had to be careful not to do too good a job at deceiving their owners, since owners who thought their slaves were not worth their cost would have found them expendable.

[5]This statement applies to the average slave. Slaves who were mistakenly asked to do more than they were capable of doing were in bad shape compared with other slaves – to the extent that they sometimes died from exhaustion.

Because their tasks were diverse, they were difficult to supervise, a difficulty that increased with the skill of the performer. Household slaves, therefore, especially skilled ones, had better opportunities to accumulate than did the slaves who worked in the fields.

The need for supervision and the desire to economize on its cost made ownership of slaves less than fully delineated. Slaves were able to capture some of these undelineated rights – in this case, rights to themselves. Success, partly due to skills in feigning inability on the one hand and to activities such as fishing on the other, and partly due to the luck of having errors made in their favor, eventually enabled some slaves to buy their own contracts.

SLAVES' CONSUMPTION

The sharp conflict between slaves' and owners' interests was not confined to slaves' effort and its supervision; it also affected consumption practices. Owners could not drive their slaves hard unless they made sure that they were properly maintained – that the nutrition, medical care, and other services slaves received were commensurate with the effort required of them. Correspondingly, in the United States, as Fogel and Engerman (1972) show, slaves received what appears, by nineteenth-century standards, to have been good medical care and a nutritious diet.[6] Owners, however, had little incentive to let their slaves consume food other than that included in the least-cost diet or to let them consume other services beyond the lowest-cost ones required for maintenance. Slaves, on the other hand, were not necessarily harmed when their productivity was lowered. Obviously, they preferred more palatable food, which they would have substituted, in part, for less pleasant if more nutritious food. One major tool owners possessed for minimizing maintenance costs was the ability to control consumption directly; they attained this control by simply providing consumption items in kind rather than allowing slaves a budget, which would have permitted choice. Thus, slaves' diet in the American South contained much corn and sweet potatoes, then considered nutritious but less desirable than the more expensive wheat and white potatoes even poor free farmers chose to consume. Owners' control of slaves' consumption, however, was not absolute. Slaves would, on occasion, avoid taking medicine, since in their eyes remaining ill was sometimes preferable to returning to work. Slaves also traded food rations for alcohol on occasion. Owners not only refrained from supplying alcohol but, most tellingly, also took various costly steps to deny slaves

[6]Fogel and Engerman, however, do not interpret their findings on nutrition the way I do. In general, they do not systematically apply transaction cost notions to the analysis of slavery.

access to it. Drinking reduced slaves' productivity, and owners made a concerted effort to make drinking expensive to slaves.

ENFORCING PROPERTY RIGHTS
IN THE PRESENCE OF SLAVERY

The legal ban on both forced slavery and voluntary slavery is now universal; in other eras, various restrictions were placed on both practices. Voluntary slavery is a contractual arrangement into which neither party would enter if she or he did not expect to gain from it. Forced slavery is an arrangement from which owners obviously gain. Nevertheless, because of problems of theft, the institution of slavery, both voluntary and forced, may entail costs that free persons might consider excessive. Two forms of theft are associated with the institution of slavery. Already mentioned is the fact that theft was the initial step in forced slavery. The other form of theft occurred when slaves escaped; the escape turned what were to their owners valuable assets into assets deprived of some or all of their value. The prohibition of slavery constituted the attenuation of individuals' rights. The gains from extending such rights, however, must be weighed against the costs associated with theft.

Coercion of free people into becoming slaves has largely been a consequence of raids and of full-fledged wars among nations. For many centuries West Africa was subject to raids and was the main source of the slaves of the American South, of the Caribbean, and of South America. Since losers of wars and raids were not the winners' countrymen, one would not expect states to outlaw that source of slavery.

Slavery was permitted at certain times and places and prohibited at others; it is not easy to explain why. I offer one highly speculative hypothesis involving policing costs: As the costs to the police of identifying and freeing forcibly enslaved free people and of recapturing escaped slaves increased, the likelihood that slavery would be prohibited was enhanced.

Raids in which free persons are captured and turned into slaves against their wills can occur within a country. Free persons will take steps privately to protect themselves against enslavement; they will also use the state to enhance their rights. The most obvious such use of the state machinery is to make enslavement of one's countrymen a crime. A more extreme step is to prohibit slavery altogether.[7] Enslaved persons would have found it exceedingly difficult to demonstrate that they were forced into slavery in a society that permitted slavery. The returns to such theft,

---

[7] The colonization of Africa probably contributed to the decline in slavery. Enhancement of property rights within colonies increased the colonies' value to the colonizers.

82

then, are higher where slavery is permitted than they are where slavery is prohibited. Conversely, the threat to free persons of being turned into slaves is relatively low in countries that prohibit slavery.[8] The fear free people have of being turned into slaves may explain, at least in part, the ban on slavery.

A rather different argument applies in the case of escaping slaves. It seems to be generally true that certain costs of protecting property from theft are assumed by the state. In Chapter 7 it will be suggested as a general proposition that activities will be banned if the police protection they require is very costly as compared with the activities' private value. If, as compared with the private value of slavery, the cost to the police of recovering escaped slaves was excessive, slavery would be banned.

The higher the danger to a country's residents of being forced into slavery and the higher the cost of recovering escaped slaves, the more likely it is that slavery will be prohibited. For a long time in the American South, being a slave and being black were almost synonymous.[9] Free people, nearly all of them white, did not have to fear becoming enslaved, and escaped slaves could readily be identified and captured. As the population of free blacks grew, however, the distinction between a free person and a slave became more difficult to make.[10] Consequently, the costs of slavery were increased, and the net gain from the institution declined.[11] If slavery were legalized in our own society, the distinction between free people and slaves would be more difficult to make and the problems of the forced enslavement of free people and of capturing escaped slaves would be even more acute than they were in the old South. It is not surprising, then, that in many societies slavery was severely restricted and that it is now prohibited everywhere.[12]

The demise of indentured servitude may have been due to forces similar to those that brought the demise of slavery. At its inception, the population in America was sparse, and servants were easily distinguished from

[8]Isolated cases of slavery are, neverthless, reported every once in a while in the contemporary press.

[9]The identification of slaves with a particular people is the apparent source of the term "slave." To the Slavs, the term "Slav" apparently meant "person." In ancient Rome, most of the Slavs present were slaves, and the Romans used the term for one to identify the other.

[10]Southern states imposed various restrictions on manumission, perhaps in order to prevent the formation of enclaves of free blacks. These efforts were not entirely successful.

[11]Some slaves who were in fact freed by their owners chose to retain the legal status of slave, presumably to retain the owners' protection and to reduce the chance of being forced back into slavery.

[12]According to Jewish law, Jews were allowed to keep other Jews as slaves but had to release them during the Sabbatical year, thus increasing the cost of turning a free person or a voluntary slave into a forced slave.

free people. With time, the population grew and diversified, making escape easier and perhaps also making the enslavement of free people easier, thus lowering the net benefit of the institution to the originally free population.

By the end of the nineteenth century, slavery had largely been abolished, perhaps because the costs of policing the institution exceeded its gains. The current prohibition of slavery implies that each individual is the owner of the capital asset embedded in her or him. The abolition of slavery was accompanied by the transfer of such capital assets from the previous slave owners to the slaves themselves. The prohibition of slavery also entails additional restrictions on contracting: Essentially, when workers contract for the supply of their own labor services, only short-term contracts are legally enforceable. These additional restrictions may also reflect the attempt to make the theft of people more costly.

SUMMARY

Even though forced slaves seem to have been stripped of any rights, in practice ownership over them was not complete. Owners had to spend resources on supervising slaves' work effort and consumption pattern and on preventing their escape. Such efforts were subject to increasing costs, and attempts to economize on these costs included granting slaves various rights. In some cases, slaves' output rather than their effort was supervised. The attempt to lower the cost of supervision then included granting slaves the right to part of the output or of their own time. These slaves, though legally their masters' property, were able to accumulate wealth and occasionally to buy their own contracts.

7

Reconciling restrictions on property rights with maximization of rights' value

Economists concerned with property rights often consider any restrictions on those rights, called "attenuations of rights," to be undesirable. A person's ability to realize the potential value of her or his property depends on the extent of her or his property rights, which consist of the ability to use (and to exclude), to alienate, and to derive income from the property. The ability, or power, to exclude prevents the property from becoming common property, and the ability to alienate and to derive income permits the realization of gains from exchange.[1] Since restrictions in general reduce freedom of action, restrictions on a person's property rights reduce the value of the property to its owner, making such restrictions appear to be harmful.

Restrictions, that is, non-price allocations, can have no useful role in the Walrasian model. In that model, only prices are needed to direct all resources into their highest-value uses. Since Walrasian price adjustments are costless, prices alone can yield efficient allocation. Restrictions, then, are at best superfluous and may well result in lower output. Economists' unfavorable attitude toward restrictions on, or attenuation of, rights may reflect the application of the Walrasian model.

In spite of the Walrasian model, however, restrictions on persons' freedom to do what they wish with "their" property are widespread, even in capitalist, market economies. For instance, store owners are sometimes prohibited from opening at night or on Sunday; automobile operators are not allowed to carry paying passengers unless they acquire a "medallion"; owners of water rights in the western United States are not free to sell the water to others or to divert it to new uses; and the size and location of structures that may be erected on urban lots are restricted by zoning regulations.

[1] The terms of alienation – whether price discrimination is legally permitted, whether sale is subject to price control, and how easily buyers can collude when dealing with the seller – may be added to this list of rights.

In these examples, the government imposes the restrictions; but restrictions are not the exclusive domain of government. Some landowners are subject to private covenants – restrictions superimposed on those of governmental zoning; and stockholders who own corporations are severely restricted as to what they may do with their properties. These two sets of private, voluntary restrictions were imposed by the original developers of such projects. The developers presumably believed that the restrictions would increase the net value of the projects to their buyers, thereby increasing the total net amount they themselves could extract. If this is so, the apparent inconsistency between wealth maximization and ownership restrictions must be just that – apparent and not real.

DIVIDED OWNERSHIP AND RESTRICTIONS ON OWNERS

As I stated in previous chapters, commodities may be viewed as collections of numerous attributes whose levels tend to vary from one specimen of a commodity to another. Individuals sometimes choose to divide the ownership of commodity attributes among themselves because the most efficient owner of one attribute is not necessarily the most efficient owner of other attributes of the same commodity. When different attributes of a commodity are owned by different individuals, a special effort is required to exclude each of them from using attributes belonging to any of the others. One way to effect exclusion is to impose restrictions on the ways owners may exercise their rights such that the commodities cannot become common property too easily. As viewed here, then, one function of restrictions on commodity ownership is to secure rights better by making exclusion easier to enforce. Such restrictions do not attenuate rights, because they tend to prevent non-owners from consuming those attributes that belong to persons other than the apparent owner.

The way a refrigerator is owned is a straightforward, convenient example of the role of divided ownership and of the corresponding restrictions. The sale of refrigerators to final consumers does not constitute an outright transfer, since the manufacturers retain responsibility for – that is, they remain the owners of – the attributes that are subject to warranty and those for which they are liable.[2] Clearly manufacturers are more efficient owners than are consumers of the potentially lethal escape of the coolant, because it is their actions during the manufacturing process that largely determine whether the coolant will escape. Manufacturers are also the more efficient owners of the motors' longevity. The longevity of motors depends, to a great extent, on manufacturing procedures about

[2]To the manufacturers, ownership generates streams of income that have only zero or negative values. Payments to the manufacturers for these potential services come ahead of time, when the original transactions are concluded.

which manufacturers are informed at a low cost and consumers are informed not at all. Refrigerator buyers, then, become the owners of only a subset of refrigerators' attributes; they do not acquire ownership of attributes such as "escape of coolant." The advantage of divided ownership comes to the fore when alienation is desirable. This is the case not only when a new refrigerator is transferred from manufacturer to wholesaler to retailer and ultimately to consumer; it is also desirable when a used refrigerator is offered for sale.

Consumers who decide to sell their refrigerators will transfer to buyers only those attributes that they own. If they were the owners of the attribute "escape of coolant," they would encounter difficulties in arranging a sale contract, since they would be able to provide satisfactory information about that attribute only at a high cost to themselves. The manufacturers, on the other hand, who are the efficient owners of "escape of coolant," remain liable for it; they continue to own this attribute. The refrigerator owners are, therefore, not involved with the transfer of the "escape of coolant" attribute, and the sale of those remaining refrigerator attributes that are easier to alienate is correspondingly facilitated.

When ownership of a commodity – a physical entity – is divided, the owners of some commodity attributes may have easy access to attributes of the same commodity that are owned by the others and may be able to treat them as free. For instance, buyers of a guaranteed product are likely to be less careful with it than they would be were it not guaranteed; to them, the service covered by the guarantee becomes a free attribute. In Chapter 3 I showed, through a discussion of the tenancy contract, how restrictions can reduce the costliness associated with free attributes. Restrictions seem to play a similar role here. For instance, refrigerator manufacturers retain ownership of liability and warranty attributes only if consumers submit to restrictions on such things as abuse and commercial use. Such restrictions help to isolate the attributes owned by the manufacturers from encroachment by consumers, thereby lowering dissipation, or capture, costs. Consumers' ownership of refrigerators is attenuated by such restrictions: Those who use their refrigerators commercially stand to lose the warranty protection. When a warranty is voided because the warrantied product is being used commercially, a consumer is being penalized for failing to heed a restriction. Not attenuated is consumers' ownership of, for instance, the right to decide what foods to store in the refrigerator; they own this particular attribute. Indeed, because the restriction on commercial use reduces capture costs, it increases the net value of the original transaction; in other words, it increases the value of the remaining attributes.

Restrictions must be enforced in order to be effective; such enforcement is costly, but not uniformly so. Damage due to commercial use of refrigerators, for instance, can be easily demonstrated; therefore, manufacturers make the warranty conditional on no commercial use. Plain carelessness is too expensive to police, and careless behavior is not restrained. The other side of this coin is that the duration of the warranty is shortened when careless behavior is expensive to police – paint on refrigerators is guaranteed for a much shorter time than motors.

The value of a transaction is another factor that helps to determine whether constraints will accompany it. In low-value transactions, the cost of managing restrictions can easily exceed the associated gains. As the value of transactions increases, it is expected that more restrictions will be imposed and that more resources will be devoted to their enforcement. Not surprisingly, both the manufacture and the use of commercial airplanes are associated with more restrictions than are the manufacture and the use of automobiles. Airlines, as a rule, contract for the manufacture of specifically designated airplanes and station their own engineers with the manufacturers. Airplane manufacturers, in turn, keep close track of the airplanes they have produced after they are delivered to airlines.

PRIVATE RESTRICTIONS AND THE COST OF POLICE PROTECTION

Restrictions on ownership may perform another function, one related to the protection of assets against theft. Because assets are always in danger of being stolen, ownership is never entirely secure. Theft can take many forms, and protection is also multidimensional. The state, through the police and the courts, provides protection against theft. The state, however, is not necessarily the most efficient protector against all aspects of theft. Car owners, for instance, can protect their cars cheaply by parking in lighted areas and by not leaving the engines running. They can also buy protection in the market by parking in lots with attendants.

Two features of state provision of policing services bear on the question of how to lower the resource cost of protection. One is that the state commits itself to assist in protection against theft; the other is that police services are supplied at no marginal charge to individuals. Individuals, then, may attempt to reduce their own efforts at protection and rely primarily on the police, even where the returns on their activities do not justify the associated costs of policing or where they can provide protection at a lower cost than the police can. The state can reduce such excessive use of police services by imposing certain restrictions on individuals. Accordingly, the state stipulates that automobiles must be equipped with locks and that individuals must lock their cars when they leave them.

The next three sections will be devoted to the interpretation, in light of the preceding discussion, of three sets of restrictive practices. Restrictions imposed by the government on water ownership in the western United States is the subject of the next section; the section after that is concerned with government restrictions on homesteaders; and a third section discusses private restrictions imposed on two firms, one that turns Chrysler hardtops into convertibles and one that is engaged in the long-term storage of a truck manufacturer's replacement parts.

RESTRICTIONS ON WESTERN WATER OWNERS [3]

Two distinct legal doctrines govern the use of water in the United States. In the East, the prevailing system is riparian, permitting landowners reasonable use of water from rivers that run by their properties, and originates from English common law. Water is relatively abundant in that region (as in England), and so naturally the rights to it are rather loosely defined. In the West, the prevailing system is appropriative, granting individuals the rights to water. The flow of water in western streams varies significantly seasonally and annually. Priorities to these streams' water are relatively clearly defined.[4] The more thorough delineation of rights to water in the West is consistent with its aridity and with the correspondingly higher value of water there. The rest of this section is concerned with restrictions on water ownership in the West.

The ownership of rights to water in the western states is most severely regulated. Individual states prevent owners from using water for purposes other than the one it originally served; the owners of rights to water are not allowed to sell them unless the sale includes the land where the water is used, and they are not free to use the water on their own properties any way they wish.

The recognition that the commodity "water" is, like other commodities, composed of many attributes is crucial if one is to understand why owners of water are not allowed to do whatever they wish with it, and why their rights are attenuated. Consider a person whose rights to a stream's water are of a relatively low priority. Only if there is enough water in the stream to meet the cumulative rights of those with higher priorities will she or he receive any. Whether or not the individual receives water depends, in part, on how much water owned by individuals with greater seniority seeps back into the stream, in other words, on what portion of the water withdrawn by those with higher priorities is returned

---

[3]This section relies heavily on Miller (1985).

[4]The priorities reflect the initial order of the individual claims on water in the streams. The amount of water originally granted to individuals was in accord with the amount actually used in their operations, usually farming. As is brought out in the next section, individuals' participation in rights protection seems easier when one owns just what one uses.

to the stream. One person's realized right to water depends on the mode others take of exercising their own rights.

Were measurement costless, individuals would presumably be granted rights to remove a certain net amount of water from a stream. A person with a right to 100 units of water could, for instance, withdraw 250 units to irrigate a crop if it was clear that 150 units would seep back into the stream. Measurement, however, is not costless; it is much cheaper to measure the amount of water removed from a stream than it is to measure the amount returned to it by seepage. Similar considerations apply to other attributes of water. It is easier to measure attributes such as salinity and temperature for the water withdrawn from a river than it is to measure the same attributes for the water in the return flow.[5]

The owners of the originally granted water rights presumably intended to use the water for a specific purpose, to irrigate an orchard, for example. The precise meaning of the grant of a low-priority right is a function of what the higher-priority holders are allowed to do. People with rights to withdraw from a stream who are restricted to a specific use of the water have rights that are delineated more narrowly than they would be in the absence of the restriction; as a result, the rights of those people with lower priorities are more clearly delineated. The more clearly rights in general are delineated, the more they are valued, because less is expected to be spent on their capture.

Two observed practices lend support to the hypothesis that the restriction on water use is intended to increase the value of water rights. The first regards interorganization transfer of water. Mutual ditch companies and irrigation districts are permitted to use water in a way that seems to evade the regulation of water transfer. These organizations of neighbors are permitted to combine the water rights of their members, thereby avoiding, within each organization, the restriction on transfers. Provided that the pattern of water use is not altered, however, the return quantity (and quality) of the water is not altered either. The loophole available to these organizations, then, does not significantly impinge on the rights of others. Allowing water transfer within ditch companies and within irrigation districts is therefore consistent with the explanation that the purpose of the more general constraint on transfers is to allow for a clear delineation of rights.

The second practice concerns the distinct form of the constraint on

[5]Because it is easier to measure the volume of water than it is to measure some of its other attributes, it is relatively easy to see to it that a reduction by one owner of the amount of water returned to the stream will not reduce the amount of water available to higher-priority owners. But a reduction in the quality of returned water will tend to reduce the water quality available to all those downstream, regardless of their priority to the water.

water use that is applied in New Mexico. In that state, water rights are defined in consumption terms – in terms of the net amount of water retained by the owner. Among the western states, New Mexico is one of the most arid, and it values its water highly, so it is not surprising that it finds the costs of the added measurement that consumption rights entail to be worthwhile. The relative ease with which owners of water rights in New Mexico may obtain the regulator's permission to sell water is consistent with the interpretation that constraints play a role in better delineating rights.[6]

HOMESTEADING

In the colonial United States, which existed before 1776, all land was initially declared to be the property of the British Crown. British authorities employed various methods of dispensing land, including granting it to states, to trading companies, and to individuals who crossed the Atlantic. The transfer of power in 1776 was accompanied by a change in the land-release policy. The U.S. federal government adopted a more unified policy of managing its land holdings, one element of which was to discourage "preemption" – the priority right of the illegal settlers, or squatters, to buy the land on which they had settled.

Until the Louisiana Purchase in 1803, most U.S. government–owned land was in the thirteen original states, and market sales of government land were routine. During the nineteenth century the U.S. government took possession of vast amounts of land in the West. Abundant as the land was, the government made a concerted effort to prevent its becoming common property. As the population grew, the government released blocks of land for settlement. These newly opened tracts of land were not, however, handled in a conventional commercial fashion. The government could have auctioned off parcels of land or set a price (or a price structure) at which to sell whatever acreage buyers wanted to purchase; instead, in various acts, best known of which is the 1862 Homestead Act, it either set a price substantially below market price or charged no price at all. At the same time it imposed severe constraints that those claiming land had to satisfy before they could gain the right to sell the land.

A possible explanation for these government restrictions is that they were imposed in order to induce settlers' self-protection against raids where such protection was cheaper than direct protection by the state. Had all unsettled land been placed in the public domain or been made available for sale so that anybody could have settled in any unoccupied

[6]Johnson, Gisser, and Werner (1981) discuss water rights in New Mexico in a similar vein.

area, the cost to the state of protecting settlers would have been high. Such costs, particularly in isolated or hostile areas, could have exceeded the net value of the newly settled areas to their owners. The total cost of protecting an area, and especially the cost to the government, would have been lower in areas abutting ones already settled.

Whereas the government seems routinely to take upon itself the protection of its people and their property, the government, as the *owner* of the land, could relatively easily have withheld protection from areas it chose to keep unoccupied. By categorizing whoever was occupying empty land as an interloper or a squatter, the government ensured that it did not have to protect such people. Because the government was the owner of the land, the decision as to whether an area was valuable enough to justify its settlement was its own. It could, then, have taken into account the cost of protection in determining whether to open a new area for settling.

The restrictions associated with homesteading, particularly those imposed by the 1862 act, are consistent with the hypothesis that their function was to induce self-protection. It is clear that dense settlement enhances self-protection. Correspondingly, a central feature of homesteading was for the government to select a unit of land – 160 acres – large enough to support a family, and to restrict each settler to one such unit.[7] A less obvious, but equally important, feature was the attempt to ensure that the land would actually be densely occupied. This may help explain not only the low (zero in the 1862 act)[8] pecuniary price of the land but also the federal government's policy of waiting to open new land for homesteading until the land became so valuable that a large fraction of the units open for homesteading had a good chance of being claimed.[9] This underpricing policy is probably what generated the excitement associated with the opening of new lands.[10] Two additional constraints were imposed on homesteaders: (1) that they actually occupy the homestead for at least five years and (2) that they improve the land before acquiring

---

[7]In later acts applying to the more arid land farther west the unit was increased to up to 640 acres.

[8]Settlers, however, could preempt the land for $1.25 per acre after six months' residence.

[9]This argument parallels Cheung's (1977) own regarding the phenomenon of owners "underpricing" the better movie theater seats in order to get those seats fully (or densely) occupied, thereby securing effective policing by the patrons themselves.

[10]All homesteads were released by the government under the same set of constraints even though they were not all equally valued. Allocation of individual homesteads was on a first-come, first-served basis, allowing the earliest claimer to claim the best homestead. In order to get a head start, some jumped the gun; hence the term "Sooner." The other side of the coin is that the lowest-value homesteads remained unclaimed. The Graduation Act of 1854 provided for progressive price reductions for such unclaimed land.

the right to sell it.[11] These two restrictions are consistent with the objective of dense settlement: They make leaving costly. The limited duration of these requirements presumably reflects the desire of the government to enhance efficient cultivation – to permit holdings of an efficient size[12] and an efficient level of labor input.

One major remaining puzzle concerns the price charged by the government for homesteads. The government could have waited to open new land until the land's net value, subject to whatever restrictions the government deemed desirable, was highest and then charged a positive price for it. By pricing the land at a zero (or near zero) pecuniary price, the government also reduced the land's net value to homesteaders, at least to the marginal ones, to zero. Pricing the land at zero is equivalent to putting it in the public domain. Thus sacrificed was the maximum amount individuals would have bid for the land. A possible explanation of such government action is that the dense settlement of a new area had an effect on the land value of neighboring settled areas. Such older areas became more secure with the settlement of the newly created buffers between them and the "empty" areas from which raiders could attack. This reduced the costs of protecting these older areas and increased their value.[13]

PRIVATE CONSTRAINTS, MAXIMIZATION, AND VERTICAL INTEGRATION

Making convertibles for Chrysler[14]

In the last two sections I attempted to explain the role of governmental constraints on private ownership. The constraints discussed in this section are strictly those between private parties. In 1984, and most likely in other years too, Chrysler contracted with another firm to turn its automobiles into convertibles. That firm did not act as a subcontractor; it purchased the auto bodies from Chrysler and then performed the conversion. By purchasing the auto bodies, the conversion firm presumably became owner of these automobiles; nevertheless, its ownership was severely constrained. First, the contract between the two firms stipulated that only Chrysler could purchase the converted cars. Second, the repurchase terms

[11]In Canada, too, homesteaders were required to occupy and improve the land before they acquired the right to alienate it.
[12]The size of the individual holding and the consolidation of holdings presented particularly acute problems where the land was used for grazing, which requires large blocks of land.
[13]However, since the initial value of an area just opened to homesteading depended on the added protection expected from future settlement, the puzzle of zero pricing remains.
[14]The information in this section was provided to me in casual conversation.

were stipulated ahead of time; Chrysler agreed to buy only cars whose conversions met its specifications, at a price set in advance. Finally, the conversion firm guaranteed the conversion; when selling the convertibles to the public, Chrysler guaranteed them but turned guarantee work concerning the conversion over to the conversion firm. It may appear, then, that the rights of the conversion firm were attenuated. Upon further examination, however, it becomes clear that the restrictions effectively delineated ownership.

The constraints Chrysler imposed on the conversion firm provided the latter with a strong incentive to perform the conversion efficiently. It would have retained any cost reduction it was able to effect and would have lost the value of cars that could not meet the repurchase specifications. The success of such vertical disintegration must have hinged crucially on the transactors' ability cheaply to measure the conversion-related attributes of both the cars Chrysler first sold and those it later repurchased.[15] Relative ease of measurement of these attributes permitted the conversion firm to become, in fact, the owner not of whole cars but of the conversion attributes of these cars. The restrictions, then, far from attenuating the rights of the conversion firm, permitted that firm to become owner of a subset of attributes and then to assume the consequences of its own operations, thereby largely removing its incentive to shirk.

Storing truck parts

For several years, Sajac, a firm specializing in long-term storage, stored spare parts made by Paccar for the Kenworth and Peterbilt trucks Paccar manufactured. The contract between Paccar and Sajac stipulated, among other things, that

1. Sajac would pay Paccar the scrap price for the parts
2. For a four-year period after receiving a batch of parts, Sajac would make the parts available to Paccar only
3. Beyond the four-year-period, Sajac would have the option of scrapping the parts or continuing to store them and to make them available to Paccar
4. For parts Paccar ordered back from Sajac, Paccar would pay 90 percent of the accounting cost
5. Paccar could refuse to accept parts it determined not to be in good condition

---

[15] It may seem that the conversion firm was earning quasi rents capturable by Chrysler. If measurement of the pertinent magnitudes is indeed easy, then disputes can be decided in the courts relatively cheaply. Under such circumstances, capture of such quasi rents does not pose a serious problem.

Reconciling restrictions with value maximization

This arrangement was quite advantageous to Paccar for income tax purposes, since the Internal Revenue Service (IRS) had stipulated a few years before that firms such as Paccar could not write off the cost of parts they did not actually sell. By selling the parts to Sajac at just a fraction of the accounting cost of these parts, Paccar was able to write these parts off. The IRS, however, challenged Paccar's write-off of the parts transferred to Sajac, claiming that the transaction did not constitute sale, because sale requires a change of ownership, and conditions such as numbers 2–5 ensured that Paccar would remain true owner of the parts.

The view that commodities are made of many attributes and that it is sometimes advantageous not to have a single person or a single firm own all the attributes suggests that there is no definitive answer to the IRS challenge.[16] Paccar did remain the owner of some attributes of the parts, but Sajac became the owner of others, namely the storage attributes. Sajac's gains came primarily from lowering the costs of storage and from selling the parts back to Paccar. Sajac apparently made efforts in both respects – it maintained facilities for low-cost, long-term storage, and it devoted resources to bring the availability of various parts to the attention of Paccar's main divisions.

It seems that Paccar's main objectives in restricting Sajac to selling the parts back were to maintain its own reputation and to prevent Sajac from taking a ride on the Paccar brand name by selling to truck drivers low-quality parts bearing Paccar's name. Paccar could have protected its brand name by storing the parts directly or by renting space from Sajac in which to store the parts, thereby retaining control of their quality. In neither case would the incentives for efficient storage have been as strong as they were in the actual case where the reward, on the margin, belonged entirely to the firm in charge of the storage.

Vertical relationships

The relationship between Paccar and the storage firm (and between Chrysler and the conversion firm) sheds light on the problem of vertical integration. Like other firms, both Paccar and Chrysler are only partly vertically integrated. In our daily life we are so used to observing highly integrated firms[17] that we fail to ask why it is that not every individual operates as an "independent," one-person firm. The preceding discussion of the relationship between the two pairs of firms points out some of the gains brought about by operating independently: When people assume ownership, they also assume responsibility for their own behavior; on the

[16]The court, however, ruled for the IRS.

[17]A supermarket, for instance, is a firm that sells a huge array of products and whose employees perform a large range of vertical (as well as horizontal) operations.

other hand, when people work as others' employees, or when other production factors are rented out, shirking is to be expected. When two
independent firms perform operations that otherwise would have been
performed within a single firm, however, exchange is required. As already argued, exchange consumes resources, and effecting full alienation
is often expensive. Correspondingly, most exchanges involve only subsets
of the attributes of the goods involved. In the case of the truck-parts
storage, Sajac, which bought the parts, seems to have operated independently of Paccar, but its operations were severely constrained. Nevertheless, these operations were much less constrained than they would have
been had they been carried out within Paccar. Sajac was more of a residual claimant to the storage operations than a Paccar division would have
been. Presumably, the costs of the partial alienation of the parts, first
from Paccar and then back to it, were relatively low; and therefore Sajac,
the storage firm, assumed responsibility for the storage operation. The
costliness of transferring other spare-parts attributes seems to be the
reason Paccar restricted Sajac to return of the parts rather than let it
dispense them without constraint.[18]

CONCLUDING REMARKS

The costliness of transacting makes undesirable side effects an almost
inevitable consequence of exchange. The ownership of commodities by
more than one person is a major source of side effects, because the owner
of a subset of a commodity's attributes can relatively easily consume
without charge some of the attributes belonging to others. It is just too
expensive, however, to price and to police all of the effects associated
with transactions. One method of reducing the costs of the attempted
capture by some people of others' rights is to impose constraints on the
former. One farmer might be able to capture another farmer's water by
switching to a crop that returns less of the withdrawn water to the
stream. The latter's rights can be protected, however, by not allowing the
former to use "her" or "his" water to irrigate new crops. Such restrictions, then, serve to enhance rights even though they may superficially
appear to attenuate them.

As the costs associated with a restriction rise, new methods of protecting rights are expected to emerge. When the value of a new crop, or the
value of the water itself, increases, I expect that protection of the rights of
lower-priority owners of water rights will be enhanced by the use of a
more expensive and more accurate method of measuring the water used

[18]The ambiguity regarding who the true owner of the parts was illustrates the
difficulty in determining what is a firm and points to the desirability of concentrating
on contracts.

by high-priority owners. The more accurate metering of the actual use of the water itself should allow indirect constraints on the use of water, such as on choice of which crops to grow to be relaxed, and will tend to grant owners of water rights greater freedom in trading their rights.

The restrictions on water use and the restrictions on homesteaders were government-imposed. The framework in which they were discussed is the same as the framework for the private restrictions Chrysler and Paccar imposed on their exchange partners. In all these cases, I assume that all decisions are ultimately made by maximizing individuals. In none of the cases are all marginal costs expected to be equated with all the corresponding marginal valuations; in all cases, however, forces toward such equalization are assumed to be present, as will be elaborated on briefly in the next chapter.

8

Property rights and non-market allocation

Those economists who have contributed most to the study of property rights tend to appreciate the operation of unregulated markets. They contend that people and the economy thrive when left to their own devices and that government intervention tends to reduce wealth. In the market, the argument goes, prices regulate the movement of resources to their highest-value uses; when prices are not given the opportunity to perform their function, misallocation results. Government intervention is deemed acceptable in such areas as national defense, police, the courts, and perhaps the money supply; however, such intervention is said to be desirable only because it facilitates the functioning of markets.

A dramatic manifestation of the view that unhindered markets are best is found in Kessel's (1974) analysis of blood donation. Although Kessel did not contribute directly to the analysis of property rights, he had a keen understanding of the property rights approach. Through an examination of the mechanisms used to provide blood where needed and of the apparent advantage donated blood has over purchased blood in avoiding the transmission of hepatitis, he came to the conclusion that a more vigorous pursuit of profit would have secured high-quality blood in the market. Yet, in spite of his masterful command over theory and evidence, Kessel's explanation as to why the market for blood had difficulty functioning and surviving is not compelling. A fuller recognition of non-market organization, that is, of the allocation of resources by mechanisms other than price, will provide a different explanation of why the quality of donated blood is higher than that of purchased blood.

The property rights approach to the study of economics was promoted by market-oriented economists, who sometimes used it to demonstrate the superiority of the market. Contrary to the perception that property rights tools may be best used to analyze the market economy, where allocation is performed largely if not entirely by prices, these tools seem, in fact, to be uniquely well suited to analyze resource allocation in non-market settings. The Walrasian approach, where rights are perfectly defined, is correct in quickly dispensing with the topic of property rights, for there is little to say about them within that model, prices being all-determining. Indeed, the Walrasian model may provide satisfactory answers to many problems in capitalist economies, where prices play a vital role in economic life.

For non-market economies, where market prices are eschewed or suppressed, the Walrasian model is inadequate: It is incapable of explaining how resources are allocated. Here, the property rights approach attains the utmost importance in the analysis of decisions about allocation. The irony is great, for champions of the free market have developed tools that are most powerful when they are used to analyze non-market, including socialist, economies.[1] Although I believe that the property rights approach applies to all human behavior and to all human institutions, I will not make a serious attempt to demonstrate this. In support of the assertion I shall, however, first offer a brief discussion of the applicability of the property rights approach to two specific areas of non-market allocation: (1) allocation by voting in market settings where it is shown that individuals sometimes choose to bypass market for non-market allocation and (2) allocation by voluntary, charitable behavior where a clear advantage of charitable over market behavior is demonstrated. I will then briefly examine the function of private property rights and the method of inducing people to perform in a non-market economy.

ALLOCATION BY VOTING

On occasion, profit-seeking individuals in market economies allocate resources by voting – an explicit mechanism that bypasses the use of prices in favor of non-price allocation. Individuals who use markets retain discretion as to how to use their wealth, maintaining full choice as to what and what not to purchase. Within voting organizations, on the other hand, individuals are subject to constraints imposed upon them by their fellow voters. Despite the reduction of their freedom of action, people must value such constraints; otherwise, such voting would not exist.

Voting is used in numerous profit-seeking settings, including shareholder corporations – mostly to elect officers; and in a whole array of operating decisions in condominiums. The origins of certain organizations in which voting is used lie in the operations of entrepreneurs. In the case of condominiums, for example, developers typically erect the housing units and related structures and complete other preparatory work

---

[1] As pointed out to me by Wing Suen, the irony is compounded by the championing of the use of prices in socialist systems by such eminent economists as Lerner and Lange.

before selling the units to individual buyers. Of course, developers do not have to sell housing units as condominiums; another option they have that maintains the owner-occupier tax advantage is to sell the units to individual buyers who operate independently of each other. In general, developers presumably do whatever they think will bring the largest difference between the aggregate selling price of their units and the costs they incur.

Developers of condominiums are, in fact, offering buyers packages that consist of both the physical structures and the rules that will govern some aspects of the prospective owners' future behavior – rules that include decisions by voting. Clearly, such developers expect to obtain higher net prices from their buyers, prices not only higher than they would be if developers sold the units independently, but also higher than they would be if developers offered different packages. Condominium buyers, then, value packages that constrain them to allocate resources by voting (on, for example, whether or not to build a swimming pool) more than they value deals that do not constrain them in that way but that allow decisions regarding the supply of such services to be made in the market.

Although no attempt is made here to explain the rationale for such behavior, it is clear that individuals sometimes prefer non-price allocation to allocation by price.[2] The use of prices, then, is not always the most efficient method of allocation. The next section, on donated blood, points to one advantage of non-market allocation.

DONATED BLOOD VERSUS PURCHASED BLOOD

Blood, like other commodities, is a collection of attributes whose individual levels vary from one specimen to another. In particular, some blood specimens are unlikely to be infected by hepatitis, and some are more likely to be infected. The lower the probability that a batch of blood is infected with hepatitis, the more valuable it is and the higher the price demanders would pay for it. By simply posting the two prices at which they would be willing to buy the two types of blood, however, buyers would be unlikely to secure the desired qualities. Since sellers prefer selling their products at higher prices, blood buyers need to be able to determine which grade of blood they are getting if they wish to avoid paying the higher price for the inferior commodity. In the time period

---

[2]Developers who construct housing units in unincorporated areas, to be sold as condominiums and to be managed by a homeowners' association, are basically developing whole political units. Since incorporation is an option for residents, developers presumably take into account the potential for such a development. Emerging in this case is the purely profit-motivated evolution of a political unit. Buyers implicitly choose the associated political restrictions.

investigated by Kessel, separation of the two kinds of blood was difficult, because at that time the test for hepatitis in blood was virtually worthless.

Despite the inaccuracy of tests, the knowledge of whether any blood specimen was or was not tainted with hepatitis was not always difficult to come by, because people often know (or at least suspect) when they are carriers of the disease. The problem is that impersonal markets are incapable of easily determining the quality of such a commodity as blood. Because information about blood is not costless to *all* concerned, the value of market exchanges of blood is greatly lowered. The information is free to a subset of individuals – the sellers – but the market is unlikely to extract the information costlessly, because the sellers can gain by concealing it.

Using a monetary reward to obtain the commodity "blood" happens to be particularly disadvantageous for securing hepatitis-free blood. The incidence of hepatitis among drug addicts is high because they tend to infect one another by sharing needles; these are the same individuals for whom cash for blood is a particularly attractive trade.[3] The attempt to purchase blood in the market, then, is likely to attract a relatively large proportion of carriers.[4] Obtaining blood from donors alters the selection criteria of suppliers because it tends to screen out cheaply people who know they are carriers. Would-be donors must be persuaded to donate and are appealed to on the basis of helping other human beings or, in the case of some oft-solicited churchgoers, of salvation. People who know or suspect that they are carriers and that their donation will do harm are simply expected not to donate.

Cash markets are not, of course, used by accident: They tend to economize on some of the costs of effecting exchange; the use of donors in lieu of cash markets incurs costs that tend to be absent from cash markets.[5] The costs and the gains of using markets as compared with other allocation methods, such as charity, differ across commodities. Given the difficulty of testing for the presence of hepatitis and of the HIV virus that causes AIDS, blood is one commodity for which the advantages of non-market over market allocation are evident.

Cash-market sellers' ability to gain by knowingly passing off low-quality specimens as high-quality ones is common to many commodities

[3] The fact that transacting is costly and needs facilitating suggests that cash is not as neutral as it is often thought to be. If, for example, blood sellers were paid in non-transferable tuition vouchers, it seems highly likely that the fraction of addicts among blood sellers would be less than it is when cash is the means of payment.

[4] Kessel named various methods of screening out individuals who are likely to be carriers. These methods, however, are costly. Sellers of blood, by and large, were not so screened, which implies that the costs of screening must have been too high.

[5] For instance, volunteers are not, in general, the lowest-cost suppliers of the commodity or service they donate.

besides blood. Charity, however, is not expected to be used in all such cases. The precise nature of the quality problem is likely to differ from one commodity to another, and each should generate its own charitable response.[6] Mechanisms other than charity may be more effective in securing the desired quality for some of these commodities.

Although a person's motive for choosing a charity to contribute to seems to be a matter of taste, one simple prediction can be derived: It seems reasonable to assume that, like other actions, charitable giving will expand when the gains it generates become larger. Returning to blood, it is probable that in the span of time after it was discovered that blood could be infected with the HIV virus but before effective tests for it were devised, the amount of blood donated relative to that sold for cash increased substantially.

ALLOCATION BY GOVERNMENT

The government of every country plays an important role in economic activity, and some governments' roles are enormous. All governments engage in non-business activities such as conducting foreign affairs and operating the courts, and virtually all also engage, though to varying degrees, in more businesslike activities, often conducting operations that in some other countries are run privately, usually for profit. It is occasionally argued that governments should seek profits when they manage their enterprises, and some government enterprises may seem actually to operate in that way. It is unclear, however, even when profit maximization is the stated objective of the government enterprise, who the residual claimants are.

The difficulty of identifying such individuals and the common claim that by and large government is wasteful and inefficient together suggest to many that private property rights are absent from government operations. Indeed, communist countries claim that they have abolished private property rights, at least with regard to the means of production. I shall argue that private property rights must exist in a functioning economy and even that the notion that government is inefficient cannot be correct. After some general comments on individual maximization, I will proceed to determine what can be inferred from the sheer existence of a government-run enterprise, using a city bus system as the example. I shall then consider the meaning of an arbitrary detail of its operations – the activities of bus drivers – and move on to more general aspects of the operation of such a system. I shall not inquire directly into what the proper areas for govern-

---

[6]This account does not explain what makes charitable giving operational, although it does shed light on the social value of inducing such a mode of behavior.

ment activity are; I am, rather, using a property rights approach to offer a glimpse into the way a government functions.

The assumption of individual maximization is heavily exploited in the economics literature featuring analysis of profit-seeking enterprises and private consumption. I wish to examine the implications of individual maximization for government operations. Because governments are run by people, government activity ultimately results from the interactions of maximizing individuals. Maximization immediately implies that government actions are never deliberately wasteful or capricious. If "waste" means that some individuals lose from an action from which nobody else gains, such occurrence is inconsistent with maximizing. Whoever takes some action must expect to gain from it; indeed, the perceived net gain must always be the largest available.

An action that appears to others to have been wasteful must, nevertheless, have been expected to generate a gain by the person who undertook it. Moreover, such a person must not have been able to gain more by acting differently. The resources under consideration are ultimately allocated to a particular use by whoever is in control of them. The logic behind the allocation is straightforward. Such resources have alternative uses, each with its own valuation. The ability of potential users to bid for the resources is subject to constraints: that bids be made only by citizens or by party members, or that bids take the form of lecture fees or promises of future high-paying jobs but not cash. Whatever the rationale for the constraints,[7] a maximizing controller of resources will allocate such resources to the highest bidder. The winning bid is not, in general, the same as the one with the highest value in the absence of the constraints. In this regard, resources may appear to be wasted, particularly in the eyes of those who do not know what the constraints are. Given the constraints, however, other potential users of the resources that appear to have been wasted must not have bid high enough for them. Applying this reasoning somewhat more generally, it can be concluded that the lower the perceived net gain to the individuals who have the right to undertake an action (no matter how beneficial the action is supposed to be or how large are its expected gains), the lower the chance that such an action will be taken.

In order to be able to analyze individual behavior in a government organization, it is necessary to address the relationship between private ownership and government activity. Because maximizing people will act only when they expect to gain from their actions, one must be able to determine who gains and who loses from government actions in order to connect the actions with ownership. Regarding a city bus system, one

[7]The constraints are, of course, also imposed by individuals who are maximizing.

must ask who owns it, that is, who has (at least some of) the power to consume it, to obtain income from it, or to alienate its assets or services. "The city" is not a satisfactory answer, because it does not identify the individuals who gain when the buses are running on time and lose when they are not. An answer like "the city" implies the denial that such individuals exist, and therefore implies the claim that there is no residual claimant to the operation of the bus system. Yet if nobody gains from improving the operations of the bus system and nobody loses by letting the system deteriorate, it must lie in the public domain. Because allowing the bus system to deteriorate requires less effort than maintaining it, it would cease to function if it lay in the public domain. Similarly, it cannot be true that the bus system lies in the public domain when access to its assets is constrained. For instance, in a functioning system, attempts to commandeer buses are likely to be punished. So long as the city bus system is not totally paralyzed, property rights over it must be in existence.[8] Various observed bus-system activities, which I outline in the following paragraphs, imply the existence of particular private property rights.

Simply observing that city buses take on and discharge passengers is evidence of the existence of a whole system of private rights. Employed bus drivers, for instance, will be fired unless they perform some minimal level of driving services. The drivers engage in an exchange with their supervisors, and exchanges constitute a *reassignment* of property rights. Here, the drivers acquire the right to a wage and relinquish some rights over their own selves in performing driving services.

Drivers may be asked to do more than the specified minimum. If they are to perform beyond the minimum, they must be given an incentive. Such an incentive need not be higher pecuniary pay; it may take form as a better chance of promotion, a more convenient work schedule, or an easier route. Whatever its form, however, no extra effort will be forthcoming without it. Drivers have at least some rights over themselves; they control – that is, they own the rights to – the level of effort, and they exchange rights over particular effort levels for some other rights.

Employed drivers cannot be operating in isolation. Somebody in the bus system must gain from the contract with the drivers, from inducing the drivers to perform busing services. Similarly, the mere fact that drivers are given routes to drive and schedules to maintain implies that somebody has been induced to perform these functions. It can be similarly inferred that certain individuals are induced to maintain buses; otherwise

[8]The claim that private property has been abolished in communist states and that all property there belongs to the state seems to me to be an attempt to divert attention from who the true owners of the property are. It seems that these owners also own the rights to the terminology.

the buses would not be in operating condition. As long as bus lines operate, then, each one of a whole array of people must be rewarded to perform his or her individual function. The bus system may be managed most bureaucratically and may function sluggishly. Still, some property rights must be granted to the individuals associated with it; otherwise no service whatsoever would be forthcoming.

Governments often seem to set output targets at levels such that at the margin valuations differ from costs. In communist countries such goals are often stated explicitly. One of the characteristics of the economies of communist countries is the constant shortages that arise from prices that have been set lower than is required to clear the market and from allocations that seem simply arbitrary. Government enterprises are affected by such policies in various ways. How would operations of the bus-system repair shop be run under such conditions? Presumably, from time to time the repair shop is hampered by a shortage of parts. As long as buses are running, we must conclude that individuals in the repair shop are being rewarded for getting the buses to work and that the rewards are larger when the repair-shop services are better. Repair-shop personnel, then, gain by having parts on hand and should, consequently, be willing to spend resources in order to secure them. They might, for instance, attempt to trade with the repair shop of another city's bus system or with a truck repair shop. Alternatively, they might offer a special reward to the parts producers for furnishing extra parts. Such producers, as is generally the case under price controls, are not likely to produce at full steam for the controlled-price segment of the market. They might readily be induced to expand output, however, if the reward were to exceed the control price.[9]

The details of such operations cannot be guessed from one's armchair; but whatever they may be, the discrepancies between marginal valuations and marginal costs must generate forces toward their elimination. Indeed, as shown in the Chapter 2 discussion of price controls, once the added adjustment of transaction costs is accounted for, the discrepancies must be eliminated entirely. This attainment of equilibrium simply follows from maximization. The equilibrium itself, however, is likely to differ from those reached under different sets of constraints. Given the government-imposed restrictions, the adjustment costs may be so high that the final output may lag drastically behind the corresponding market outcome.

[9]Some non-market economies are called "command" economies; a command economy is one in which the planner imposes an output target besides the control price. Because inputs are never uniform and because of random fluctuations, the target will as a rule fall short of maximum output, and some shirking with regard to the target output may also occur. The quantity supplied, then, is expected to increase if the reward is larger; an increase will not be forthcoming if it is simply commanded.

The advantages of allowing residual claimants to operate in an economy are clear. In the context of new opportunities for the bus system, suppose it is recognized that the residents of a new suburb are willing to pay more for bus services than these services would cost. If an individual were in charge of the decision whether or not to start service and if she or he were also the sole claimant to the residual, the service would be provided because the individual would reap the difference between the gains and the cost. Moreover, such a service would be expanded until, on the margin, the cost equaled the gain.

In a political system, given the way such systems usually operate, the effect of demand forces is less direct, but it is definitely not absent. The system of rewards in government seldom compensates individuals for the full private gains they generate. An operator unable to claim the full 100 percent of the residual would stop short of the level of service a private operator would reach. Although the same forces that bridge gaps created by price controls tend to prevent gaps between marginal valuations and marginal costs from growing indefinitely large, a full-fledged residual claimant is less handicapped than is one who has only a partial claim, and the full-fledged claimant will produce what appears to be a more efficient outcome.

Why would an operator not be allowed to claim the full 100 percent of the residual? More generally, why are individuals not always allowed free rein to become residual claimants? Prohibitions must perform real functions. The superior who has constrained the operator presumably had the power to impose constraint.[10] The superior may have had no interest in increasing the operator's wealth but could still have been able to increase her or his own wealth by selling the right to serve the suburb. Answering the question regarding the absence of a full-fledged residual claimant requires asking what prevented the superior from selling the right to the operator or, even better, to the highest bidder. The answer lies in the fact that the seller's wealth depends not only on the pecuniary price but also on features of the buyer and of the exchanged property.

Maximizers may choose not to sell an asset or a franchise to the highest bidder for a variety of reasons, several of which are implicit in the discussions of earlier chapters, and all of which may be viewed as resulting from the presence of side effects. Manufacturers, for instance, sometimes pay their salespeople a commission or a salary instead of selling them the merchandise outright. By not granting salespeople full residual-claimant status, manufacturers ensure that their incentive for capturing wealth from other salespeople is tempered. In another case, persons who cannot fully

---

[10]For simplicity, the superior here is assumed to possess the ultimate authority; people intermediate in the hierarchy are ignored.

guarantee their actions may be inclined to take unduly large risks. The incentive to undertake excessively risky projects is reduced if the decision makers are not allowed to become full-fledged residual claimants.

One reason residual-claimant rights are not granted may apply primarily to despotic regimes; it has to do with the concentration of wealth that free enterprise entails. The holders of residual claims may encounter bad luck and be impoverished, or luck may smile on them and they may become rich. When many opportunities to assume residual claims are made available, at least a few individuals are likely to become rich. Rich people, particularly when their wealth is not easy for others to keep track of, are in a position to finance coups; such people pose a threat to the despot. This, I suspect, is one reason why dictators are often averse to free enterprise. Communist regimes' harsh treatment of "profiteers" may be a case in point. The suppression of opportunities that may enrich some individuals is costly to dictators, who could instead allow their exploitation while collecting a commensurate franchise fee. It is not that dictators are not assumed to be maximizers. It is their longevity that is seen to be valuable to them. They are willing to sacrifice pecuniary gains that they could obtain by auctioning off various residual rights but that pose a risk to their security for the option of operating bureaucratically – an option that is less lucrative but that promises greater longevity.

The distinction between the private and the public sectors is not a distinction between the presence and absence of private property rights. Such rights are necessarily present in both systems. The distinction lies instead in organization, and particularly in the incentives and rewards under which producers tend to operate. In the private sector, producers are more readily given the opportunity to assume the entire direct effects of their actions. In the government sector, people assume a smaller portion of the direct effect of their actions. Both systems reflect the outcome of the actions of maximizers. Each must be efficient.

9

Additional property rights applications

In previous chapters, the property rights approach was useful in explaining various aspects of such specific phenomena as gasoline price controls and slavery and in developing a general approach to, among other things, non-market allocation, the maximizing role of restrictions on private property rights, and, in the context of farm tenancy, the choice among various contract forms. The property rights framework can be applied to various other problems. I shall consider several additional areas to which property rights notions can be applied: people's ability to protect themselves against losses to monopoly, the relationship between property rights and theft, property rights to innovations, and property rights to price information.

PROTECTION AGAINST LOSSES TO MONOPOLY

Monopolies are said to result in resource misallocation taking two forms. The first, better-known kind arises because monopolies produce "too little," charging prices that exceed marginal costs. The second kind of misallocation arises in the process of the creation of monopolies. Would-be monopolists spend resources in order to attain monopoly positions and such expenditures are dissipating. The magnitude of these capture costs is comparable to that of the expected monopoly profits. Since monopolists' gains exceed their contributions, they seem to have the right to harm other people. Yet such rights are not exercised indiscriminately, and it is of interest to determine the circumstances under which such power is used.

In general, a property that can be captured must lie, at least in part, in the public domain. Moreover, what lies in the public domain must have been relinquished by whoever previously owned it. In the case at hand, if someone is able to capture a monopoly position, or, more accurately, if someone is able to capture, at a resource cost, the rights to the monopoly gain, then the monopoly position itself must have been lying in the public domain;

and in order for these rights to have entered the public domain, people must have relinquished their rights in the first place. I will delineate conditions under which people would allow this to happen for the case in which monopoly is attained by predatory pricing. In predatory pricing, an initially competitive industry is taken over by a predator who monopolizes it by temporarily pricing the target commodity at less than it costs, thereby forcing the competitive producers either to leave the industry or to sell their facilities to the predator. This method illustrates well the general principle behind opportunities for capturing monopoly gains.[1]

Prior to predatory action, consumers were able to purchase the target commodity from many sellers at a competitive price; this ability is threatened by the predator. Since property rights are defined here as individuals' ability to gain from the consumption and exchange of goods, it seems proper to inquire what gives consumers the ability to obtain a good at the competitive price. Antimonopoly laws aside, consumers surely do not have a legal right to the competitive price. Consumers, however, can acquire the rights (in the economic sense of the term) by the simple expedient of signing long-term competitively priced contracts for the commodity. They might choose to take such action if they fear monopolization by a predator. Long-term contracts will also benefit the competitive sellers: It is difficult to ruin sellers who have signed such contracts, because they do not have to sell all their output at the predatory price; and these competitive sellers command a high acquisition price from the predator. As long as the extra costs of arranging long-term contracts over and above those of spot exchanges are less than the monopoly gain, threatened sellers and consumers will gain by establishing rights to supply and to be supplied respectively at the competitive price.[2] When the cost of protection, whether by long-term contracts or any other means, is less than the expected monopoly loss, the would-be monopolist stands to lose from the attempted monopolization. In this sense, the would-be predator does not have the right to such a gain. Assuming that in the absence of defensive action the predatory practice is a real threat to competitive buyers and sellers, it is expected that the less costly it is to arrange long-term contracts in an industry, the less likely it is that the industry will be subject to monopolization.

In summary, consumers' and competitive sellers' ability to exchange at

[1] I take no account of the controversy surrounding the logic of, and the evidence for, predatory practices.

[2] The successful predator will gain more (in present terms) from the ultimate monopoly pricing than she or he will lose from below-cost pricing during the predatory period or from buying out competitors at terms attractive to them. Conversely, consumers and preyed-on firms will be the combined net losers from such predation, and it seems highly probable that consumers' losses from the monopoly price will exceed their gains from the initial lower price.

competitive prices depends on their own efforts to enforce the appropriate arrangements. When enforcement costs are high, however, consumers' and sellers' rights to be served at the competitive price are likely to be relinquished, and a predator may then capture the right to a monopoly position.

THE RELATIONSHIP BETWEEN PROPERTY RIGHTS AND THEFT

The existence of theft makes the distinction between economic and legal rights clear; it also highlights the notion that economic rights are never absolute. Thieves lack legal rights over what they steal; nevertheless, they are able to consume it and to exclude others from it, to derive income from it, and to alienate it. Each of these capabilities is an attribute of ownership. The lack of legal rights may reduce the value of these capabilities, but it does not negate them.

The fact that thieves have rights over stolen property implies that the current owners of property that might possibly be stolen do not have full rights over "their" property. Owners cannot be certain of the future use of such properties. The rights they do have depend, in part, on the protection effort made by the state. These rights also depend on the measures owners take to protect themselves from theft; the more they spend, the more secure their rights are expected to become. These efforts are not expected to deter all theft; for instance, fences around orchards are not made to be totally insurmountable. Here, too, then, individuals choose to leave some rights in the public domain. When the probability that thieves will steal one's apples from backyard trees is positive, then one has only partial ownership over the apples.

Private protection methods are as varied as are commodities themselves. Owners of apple orchards may employ guards to reduce theft; they may place trees farther from their property boundaries than they would in the absence of theft; and they may grow less valuable apples that are less appealing to thieves. Indeed, in the absence of theft, owners might be growing entirely different crops on their land.

The notion that theft is a manifestation of the general case of imperfect delineation of rights can be illustrated further by reconsidering movie theaters. Of the attributes theater owners relinquish to the public domain, two relate to the difference in value among seats. The first relinquished attribute is the difference in value between the better and the worse seats within a price class of seats. People can capture the difference in value by arriving early and occupying the better seats. To the extent that policing is not perfect, a second attribute that is relinquished in part is the difference in value across price classes. Buyers of low-price tickets can capture the difference to the extent that they are not prevented from occupying higher-price seats. The state takes part in the enforcement effort only in the latter case, since jumping seats constitutes a legal infraction, whereas selecting a certain seat within a price class obviously does not. The economic logic of the two types of capture, however, is the same.

PROPERTY RIGHTS TO INNOVATIONS

The importance of property rights considerations to innovations has been widely recognized by economists; nevertheless, some major rights issues remain unresolved. One such issue concerns the rights innovators can expect to have over their innovations. When an innovation is developed by a uniquely talented individual, it seems plausible that such an individual will have the field to herself or himself and be able to obtain the rights to the innovations. On the other hand, if many individuals are able to develop the same innovation at similar costs, it may appear that none has a right to it and that in their competition for the gain from the innovation its economic value will be dissipated; nevertheless, in this case too rights may be well defined.

A useful measure of the net present value of an innovation is the difference between total consumers' valuation and total innovators' costs. Each of the potential patterns of activity leading to a particular innovation will generate its own net present value. The highest value will be generated by the innovation activity that satisfies two conditions: that it be free of duplication and that it be undertaken at the time that yields the highest consumers' valuation net of innovating costs. One market force that tends to bring about the realization of these conditions is competition among innovators in recruiting customers for their particular innovations before expending capital on the actual innovation.[3] In order to attract potential customers away from competing innovators, not only will innovators tend to cede to customers all the gains from the innovation, but the winning innovator will also be the one who performs the innovation activity closest to the time that maximizes its net present value; only then can the bid for customers dominate that of competitors. When the cost of recruiting customers, whether directly or indirectly, is low, customers have, in practice, the rights to the gain from the innovation. Here, as in the case of predatory practices, the easier is advance contracting, the better are rights delineated.

Innovators who possess unique talents do not need to cede to custom-

[3]Yu (1981) discusses extensively methods used for such recruiting. Demsetz (1968) was the first to consider advance contracting for selling commodities whose production is subject to declining costs.

ers all the potential gains the innovations generate. Such innovators may encounter another problem, however. Every customer may try to obtain a bargain for herself or himself by offering the lowest royalty payment. Since the innovators' marginal cost of serving extra consumers is zero, they may be willing to give ground rather than lose customers. Individuals' incentive for bargaining under these conditions implies that the difference between the maximum consumers' valuation and the marginal cost lies in the public domain. The potential loss from such bargaining can, however, be lowered if the parties can be restrained not to bargain. Therefore, if the option of selling the use of the innovation to different consumers at different prices can be taken away, either privately or by the legal prohibition of price discrimination, the innovator's rights over the innovation will be partially restored. Maximizing sellers will equate their constrained marginal revenue to their (zero) marginal cost and will price accordingly. The superimposed uniformity of prices – the royalty rates here – delineates rights, and their determination is free of direct capture costs. The arrangement is not entirely free of cost, however, because when a single price is prescribed the welfare triangle that could have been avoided under price discrimination is relinquished to the public domain.

PROPERTY RIGHTS TO PRICE INFORMATION

Economists seldom consider that to determine which prices will clear the market is a resource-consuming activity. Were such prices easy to determine, no serious errors in setting prices would occur, yet significant pricing errors are widespread. Some concerts, for example, are poorly attended, whereas for others tickets can be obtained only from scalpers; some artists sell out at their gallery openings, and others see an entire show go by without selling a thing; as a final example, some new stock offerings are instantly snatched up, and others prove to be duds. Such examples suggest that setting prices correctly is costly. Providing price estimates is costly and must generate a reward; since the estimates are subject to error, speculators may capture value. Resources will be spent, then, both on the capture of price information and on the prevention of such capture.

It is to be expected that prices will be set by individuals who specialize in this activity, but the direct sale of price estimates is problematic. Were the producers of commodities to purchase price estimates for them, they would also require a guarantee of the quality of the service they were buying. Some of these commodity producers, however, could take advantage of the fact of the guarantee by lowering product quality and shifting part of the guarantee burden to the pricing specialist. This difficulty may be avoided if the producer of the commodity also sets the price, which may explain why the two activities are often performed within the same organization.

Some commodities and services are not as susceptible to the problem of guarantee abuse as others, and for these the producer of the price estimate may guarantee her or his service, thereby becoming the residual claimant to variability in the value of the service. An important example of the provision of price services by independent specialists may be seen in syndicates of investment bankers, which advise business firms about the price at which to sell new stock. At the heart of the transaction between a syndicate and an issuer of stock is the implicit price guarantee. Essentially, a syndicate buys the entire stock flotation at the agreed-upon price and offers it to the public at a price not exceeding a predetermined ceiling. A syndicate that errs by overestimating the market-clearing price will be the one to bear the effect of its error. The syndicate, then, maintains a property right to its price estimate.

Pricing errors may have an additional effect on behavior. The ultimate buyers of a new stock may either rely on the recommendation of the syndicate or devise their own (or use their advisers') estimates of the market price of a stock and act accordingly. The latter action constitutes a duplication of effort, since the information is a public good that has already been produced by the syndicate. The demand for a stock is higher, the lower the costs associated with acquiring it; the demand is also higher if demanders believe that, on average, over many stock offerings, their suppliers offer them bargains. They cannot expect, however, that every new stock will be a bargain. Since some stocks are expected to be duds and others are expected to be bargains, buying only the latter and avoiding the former would be highly profitable. Information on new offerings that allows a speculator to avoid some of the duds while concentrating on the bargains should enable her or him to earn a positive return. Success by such a speculator, however, will lower the return to uninformed buyers; they will be forced to buy relatively more duds, since a relatively large fraction of the bargains will already have been taken by the speculator. The demand for stocks by buyers who do not acquire information on individual issues but who are aware of the average return on new stocks will be lower when they must compete with speculators, and lower stock prices will result.

In order to protect their rights from being captured by speculators and to prevent an adverse shift in the demand facing them, syndicates must deter speculators from acquiring information. This may explain the restrictions on the number of shares of a new issue individuals or organizations are allowed to purchase. If a would-be speculator can use her or his information to buy only small blocks of shares, she or he will seldom find the information worth collecting. Thus the restriction seems to protect the rights of syndicates to their costly price information.

10

The property rights model: Recapitulation

People can effect rights delineation, and as part of their maximization effort people can delineate rights to whatever degree they desire. In this sense, rights are always well delineated. Because commodities are not uniform and are costly to measure, however, perfect delineation is prohibitively costly, and so rights are never perfectly delineated.

Those properties that people have chosen not to delineate are in the public domain. Such properties include much of the world's oceans; they also include the cool air in air-conditioned shopping malls, which is not charged for on the margin. Properties in the public domain can be augmented or diminished. As the values of commodities and of commodity attributes change, and as the costs of delineation and of protection change, prople's decisions regarding what to leave in, what to relinquish to, and what to reclaim from the public domain will change correspondingly.

The public domain is ubiquitous; innumerable commodity attributes are placed in it. Any service not fully charged for on the margin is at least partly relinquished to the public domain. Owners could charge for such services, but the extra returns often do not justify the extra costs. For instance, concert-hall owners relinquish into the public domain the differential in valuation among equally priced seats. When the value of concert-hall seats falls, which happens when, for example, a famed opera star leaves the hall and a local choir begins using it, seats are expected to be priced in less detail. The differences in value among seats that were formerly differentially priced are relinquished into the public domain. Patrons are expected to claim that differential through the expenditure of resources. Resource owners attempt to maximize the net values of their resources: They attempt to organize their action so that, ceteris paribus, losses to the public domain are minimized.

Because rights to commodities are costly to delineate, some of the valued attributes of these transactions are subject to capture. In order to gain from exchange, people must spend resources on transferring rights to commodities. Contracts are expected to be structured so as to minimize the costs of exchange of given transactions. In forming their contracts, transactors have a choice of units by which to meter their transactions; for instance, labor can be exchanged by the hour or by the piece. The use of each of these units relinquishes different subsets of attributes to the public domain: the per-hour effort when labor is sold by the hour; the care, or quality of the output, when labor is sold by the piece.

In addition to having a choice of units, contractors may also impose restrictions on the way they conduct their exchanges in order to reduce the amount they spend to capture from each other. Refrigerator producers, for example, often make the sale of their merchandise subject to a warranty while requiring buyers to use their refrigerators only non-commercially. The warranty service is a free attribute to buyers in that they are not as heavily penalized for carelessness as they would be if they had to pay for repairs themselves. The restriction serves to reduce such carelessness. The more valued transactions are, the more comprehensive the restrictions are expected to be.

Since exchanged commodities are not uniform and are not fully measured, the value of the exchange is subject to variability. A contract allocates the variability in a transaction among the transactors. As transactors alter the units by which they effect exchange and as they alter the associated restrictions, they also divide the variability in outcome among themselves differently. That allocation of variability that maximizes the contractors' wealth is the one wherein the ability of a contractor to affect the value of the mean outcome of the transaction is positively related to the share of variability she or he will assume. It is expected, for instance, that refrigerator manufacturers will assume variability in income by guaranteeing most comprehensively those aspects of their refrigerators' performance most affected by their production procedures and least likely to be affected by consumers' actions. We observed that the guarantee on refrigerators' motors remains in force for several years, whereas refrigerators' paint is guaranteed for only a short period.

All sales except some of those governed by caveat emptor require organization. In sales subject to caveat emptor, buyers need assurance that they will not walk away with worthless merchandise. If buyers check directly, the degree of organization may be trivial.[1] Non–caveat emptor sales, that is, sales in which the transactors have imposed constraints on each other, require real organization in order to police and to monitor the constraints. The nature of, and the costs associated with, such organizations vary with the pricing method used. A change in conditions, such as a change in the valuation of the transacted commodity, is expected to

---

[1] Not trivial, however, is the resource cost of such exchanges.

change the method by which the commodity is sold and, with it, the organizational structure governing its exchange. Regarding which party will post the price at which exchange will be conducted, this theory yields the implication that the party who can better predict price will be the one posting prices. The seller may post a price and then agree to deal at that price, or the buyer may make the commitment. Whoever posts a price subjects herself or himself to exploitation; her or his exchange partners may engage in excessive price prediction, discover prediction errors, and take advantage of the willingness to deal at a fixed price. The implication is that the person who can more readily predict the price will be the one assuming the consequences of posting it. Thus, as the size of the buyer vis-à-vis the seller increases, the more likely are buyers (whose unit cost of prediction has declined) to post prices at which they agree to purchase what sellers wish to sell.

Because all but the lowest-value transactions are subject to constraint and require organization, only a small fraction of transactions are in the market as this term is usually understood. The accompanying oft-asked question of which transactions will take place in the market and which will remain within the firm is not likely to elicit a useful answer, however. Firm transactions are not uniform, and some of them are more in the firm than others. A more fruitful question concerns the determination of the form of organization that will govern different kinds of transactions and of the forces that will bring change to these organizations.

The complexity of commodities and activities makes ownership patterns complex as well. The most efficient owner of a particular commodity attribute is not necessarily the most efficient owner of the commodity's other attributes. It may be advantageous, then, to split the ownership of a commodity among several individuals. Because the commodity is not itself physically split, its owners may find it easy to consume some of each other's unpriced attributes if they are not properly constrained. In the just-mentioned restriction on the commercial use of refrigerators, the owner of the attribute "guarantee service" restricts the behavior of the owners of some of the refrigerator's other attributes.

Organizations that exist to police and to monitor constraints are themselves complex. Many factors affect the variability in income of an organization such as the business firm: The price of each commodity it buys or sells can fluctuate, and each specimen of the commodities it deals in may differ from others; in addition, its income may depend on whether or not such phenomena as fires, earthquakes, and foreign confiscations occur. Each of these instances of income variability may be borne by a different party. A firm may purchase a raw material on the spot market or may operate under a long-term fixed-price contract for it. Assuming no breach of contract, in the former case the buying firm bears the effect of fluctuations in the price of the commodity; in the latter case it is insured against such fluctuations. Such considerations apply to all the firm's sources of variability. It is expected here, too, that the party that is better able to affect the mean outcome will tend to assume the associated variability. For instance, it is expected that a raw-material supplier who has some power to set its price is more likely to sign fixed-price long-term contracts than is one not possessing such power.

Similar considerations apply to labor services. When workers can affect outcome value more easily than the demander of the labor services can, the labor suppliers are more likely to operate as independent contractors selling output rather than labor. At the other extreme, the demanders of labor services will assume variability in outcome by paying a fixed long-term wage. It is expected, then, that as workers' market wage rises, they will gravitate toward self-employment (Barzel, 1987).

When two parties agree to a formula for dividing future income variability, one will emerge as the winner and one as the loser. Because the loser could gain by reneging on the contract, each party demands assurances from the other that the contract will not be breached. A necessary though not sufficient condition for such assurances is that a party be able to meet her or his obligations. Fixed-wage suppliers of labor can readily guarantee performance even when the market wage exceeds the contract wage, because they own their own labor services. The employer of such workers must be able to ensure wage payment when the market wage falls below the contract wage. Equity capital specializes in providing such assurance. More generally, it seems that equity capital is assembled (and augmented) in order to guarantee all the contracts signed by the firm. These contracts may, in turn, be viewed as constituting the firm; and in this sense shareholders are the owners of the firm (and the firm is a "nexus of contracts").

CONCLUDING REMARKS

I have attempted to demonstrate how the property rights transaction cost model can generate a better understanding of the allocation of resources and of the interaction of this allocation with economic organization. The literature that assumes that the costs of transacting are zero and that all property rights are perfectly well delineated is incapable of dealing with a vast array of actual observed practices. Particularly glaring is the inability of such an approach to explain why exchange parties would ever impose restrictions on each other. The property rights approach is capable of addressing such issues; I have offered some answers.

Many approaches to the analysis of economic behavior do not explicitly assume that transaction costs are zero, but neither do they emphasize the property rights angle. It is my impression that economists who neglect property rights considerations tend to make implicit assumptions that are often not well taken and that produce hard-to-swallow results. It is quite common to find cases where within single models some transaction costs are implicitly assumed to be zero (for instance, it is routinely assumed that monopolists know precisely what their demand is) while others are assumed to be prohibitively expensive (for instance, it is routinely assumed that price discrimination by monopolists is too costly).[2] The approach that insists on asking who owns every particular attribute of a commodity and what "owners" can actually do with "their" commodities seems to come closer to the root of transaction costs and is, therefore, less prone to make untenable assumptions.

Finally, consider the application of the property rights approach to the distribution of the gains from trade. Many goods are valued less by their current owners than they are by other individuals. Who owns these potential gains from trade? In the competitive, zero transaction costs model, the distribution of the gains is costlessly determined. The costless information (or the uniformity of commodities) necessary for such competition is, however, seldom encountered in reality. Opportunities for people to gain at the expense of others seem rampant. Whereas individuals are always ready to expend resources to increase their share of the pie, they will also seek methods and organizations that better delineate rights to it and will thus divide the pie without shrinking it too much.

A sizable part of this book analyzes such behavior. It is fitting to finish by considering one unlikely place where the time and effort of haggling over the distribution of the gains from trade are effectively avoided: a Middle Eastern bazaar. In Cairo's "principal livestock market, [where] camels take center stage . . . the camel market's own King Solomon [is] Muhammad Abd al-Aziz. . . . Sales are conducted one-on-one – one buyer, one seller and one camel at a time. . . . With an acutely discriminating sense of camel flesh . . . Muhammad . . . sets a fair price. . . . His authority is usually sufficient to settle any difference." Transaction costs are near zero in this particular market. Nothing, however, comes free. Here, the cost in question is "a small margin for [Muhammad's] commission."[3]

[2]Another example occurs in asymmetry-of-information models, where one set of individuals is, as a rule, implicitly assumed to be costlessly informed while for others the information cost is assumed to be prohibitive.
[3]Werner (1987).

References

Alchian, Armen A. 1965. "Some Economics of Property Rights." *Il Politico*, 30, no. 4: 816–29. Reprinted in Armen A. Alchian, *Economic Forces at Work*. Indianapolis, Ind.: Liberty Press, 1977.

Alchian, Armen A., and William R. Allen. 1977. *Exchange and Production*, 2nd ed. Belmont, Calif.: Wadsworth.

Alchian, Armen A., and Harold Demsetz. 1972. "Production, Information Costs, and Economic Organization." *American Economic Review*, 62, no. 5: 777–95.

Arrow, Kenneth J. 1973. "Higher Education as Filter." *Journal of Public Economics*, 2, no. 3: 193–216.

Barzel, Yoram. 1974. "A Theory of Rationing by Waiting." *Journal of Law and Economics*, 17, no. 1: 73–96.

    1977. "An Economic Analysis of Slavery." *Journal of Law and Economics*, 20, no. 1: 87–110.

    1982. "Measurement Cost and the Organization of Markets." *Journal of Law and Economics*, 25, no. 1: 27–48.

    1987. "The Entrepreneur's Reward for Self-Policing." *Economic Inquiry*, 25, no. 1: 103–16.

Cheung, Steven N. S. 1969. *A Theory of Share Tenancy*. Chicago: University of Chicago Press.

    1974. "A Theory of Price Control." *Journal of Law and Economics*, 17, no. 1: 53–72.

    1977. "Why Are Better Seats 'Underpriced'?" *Economic Inquiry*, 15, no. 3: 513–22.

    1983. "The Contractual Nature of the Firm." *Journal of Law and Economics*, 26, no. 1: 1–22.

Coase, Ronald H. 1937. "The Nature of the Firm." *Economica*, 4, no. 3: 386–405.

    1960. "The Problem of Social Cost." *Journal of Law and Economics*, 3, no. 1: 1–44.

Dahlman, Carl J. 1980. *The Open Field System and Beyond: A Property Rights Analysis of an Economic Institution*. Cambridge: Cambridge University Press.

Dam, Kenneth W. 1965. "Oil and Gas Licensing and the North Sea." *Journal of Law and Economics*, 8, no. 2: 51–76.

Demsetz, Harold. 1967. "Toward a Theory of Property Rights." *American Economic Review*, 57, no. 2: 347–59.

References

1968. "Why Regulate Utilities?" *Journal of Law and Economics*, 11, no. 1: 55–66.

Fogel, Robert William, and Stanley L. Engerman. 1972. *Time on the Cross: The Economics of American Negro Slavery*. Boston: Little, Brown.

Gordon, H. Scott. 1954. "The Economics of a Common Property Resource: The Fishery." *Journal of Political Economy*, 62, no. 2: 124–42.

Hall, Christopher D. 1986. "Market Enforced Information Asymmetry: A Study of Claiming Races." *Economic Inquiry*, 24, no. 2: 271–91.

Jensen, Michael C., and William H. Meckling. 1976. "Theory of the Firm: Managerial Behavior, Agency Costs and Ownership Structure." *Journal of Financial Economics*, 3, no. 3: 305–60.

Johnson, Ronald N., Micha Gisser, and Michael Werner. 1981. "The Definition of a Surface Water Right and Transferability." *Journal of Law and Economics*, 24, no. 2: 273–88.

Kalt, Joseph P. 1981. *The Economics and Politics of Oil. Price Regulation: Federal Policy in the Post-Embargo Era*. Cambridge, Mass.: MIT Press.

Kessel, Rueben A. 1974. "Transfused Blood, Serum Hepatitis, and the Coase Theorem." *Journal of Law and Economics*, 17, no. 2: 265–90.

Klein, Benjamin, Robert G. Crawford, and Armen A. Alchian. 1978. "Appropriable Rents, Vertical Integration, and the Competitive Contracting Process." *Journal of Law and Economics*, 21, no. 2: 297–326.

Knight, Frank H. 1921. *Risk, Uncertainty and Profit*. Boston: Houghton Mifflin.

1924. "Some Fallacies in the Interpretation of Social Cost." *Quarterly Journal of Economics*, 38, no. 7: 582–606.

Krueger, Anne O. 1974. "The Political Economy of the Rent-seeking Society." *American Economic Review*, 66, no. 3: 291–303.

Miller, Kathleen A. 1985. "The Right to Use vs. the Right to Sell: Water Rights in the Western United States." Unpublished Ph.D. thesis, University of Washington.

Posner, Richard A. 1986. *Economic Analysis of Law*, 3rd ed. Boston: Little, Brown.

Rockoff, Hugh. 1984. *Drastic Measures: A History of Wage and Price Controls in the United States*. Cambridge: Cambridge University Press.

Ross, Stephen A. 1973. "The Economic Theory of Agency: The Principal's Problem." *American Economic Review*, 63, no. 2: 134–39.

Spence, A. Michael. 1973. "Job Market Signaling." *Quarterly Journal of Economics*, 87, no. 4: 355–79.

Stigler, George J. 1966. *The Theory of Price*, 3rd ed. New York: Macmillan.

Tullock, Gordon. 1967. "The Welfare Cost of Tariffs, Monopolies and Theft." *Western Economic Journal*, 5, no. 3: 224–32.

Umbeck, John. 1977. "The California Gold Rush: A Study of Emerging Property Rights." *Explorations in Economic History*, 14, no. 2: 197–206.

1981. "Might Makes Right: A Theory of the Formation and Initial Distribution of Property Rights." *Economic Inquiry*, 19, no. 1: 38–59.

Varian, Hal R. 1984. *Microeconomic Analysis*, 2nd ed. New York: Norton.

Werner, Louis. 1987. "North to Cairo Along the Scorching Way of the Forty." *Smithsonian* (March): 120–32.

Williamson, Oliver E. 1975. *Markets and Hierarchies: Analysis and Antitrust Implications*. New York: Free Press.

1985. *The Economic Institutions of Capitalism*. New York: Free Press.

Yu, Ben T. 1981. "Potential Competition and Contracting in Innovation." *Journal of Law and Economics*, 24, no. 2: 215–39.

Index